CROP CIRCLES

'The Nature of God is a circle
of which the centre is everywhere
and the circumference is nowhere'

Empedocles of Agrigentum, 490 BC

CROP CIRCLES
The Greatest Mystery of Modern Times

Lucy Pringle

Thorsons

Thorsons
An Imprint of HarperCollins*Publishers*
77–85 Fulham Palace Road,
Hammersmith, London W6 8JB

The Thorsons website address is:
www.thorsons.com

First published 1999

10 9 8 7 6 5 4 3 2 1

A catalogue record for this book
is available from the British Library

ISBN 0 7225 3855 3

Printed and bound in Great Britain by
The Bath Press, Bath

Contents

Foreword

It is a pleasure and a privilege to have been invited by Lucy Pringle to write a Foreword to her book *Crop Circles – The Greatest Mystery of Modern Times*.

There must be very few people who have never heard of crop circles, those enigmatic patterns that have appeared for many years in fields of cereal crops in a number of locations throughout the world. Most of those people who do know of them, though formerly interested and intrigued by such events and the subsequent media feeding frenzy, would, if asked, admit to assuming that the crop circle saga came to an end years ago, that it had been established that the circles had been hoaxed by – who was it? Bill and Ben the Flower-Pot Men? or something like that; interest in the subject had by now surely evaporated though a few circles were still tramped out each summer by pranksters or agri-artists, motivated to show how easy it was to create even complicated formations and display the monumental gullibility of a few simpletons who still believed in them.

So why yet another book on the subject?

First, let me state my interests in the matter.

About ten years ago, Lucy Pringle, Michael Green, the late Ralph Noyes, Richard Andrews, Busty Taylor, Leonie Starr, the Earl of Haddington, Beth Davies and a few other interested souls like myself, spent a weekend sharing our personal experiences of crop circle phenomena. It was a most pleasurable two days and a revelation of the number of people, following a wide diversity of sober professions, who had become fascinated by those beautiful, haunting circles that had been appearing overnight in greater and greater numbers in fields of wheat, oats, corn, oilseed rape so suddenly, so unexpectedly and so mysteriously. We found that all of us, in our various ways, wanted to understand why they appeared. Apart from their beauty, was there anything significant to be found in their shapes and construction? And so, encouraged by our mutual interest and sincere motivation, we formed the Centre for Crop Circle Studies (the CCCS).

Of course we were not the first people to study the circles, though some of us, like Busty Taylor, had been doing so for years. Others, like Colin Andrews, Pat Delgado and Terence Meaden, have been measuring and photographing the circles long before the CCCS was formed and trying to provide a reasonable theory to explain their appearance. There was indeed no shortage of theories. There were almost as many theories as there were people interested in the phenomenon. Fraud (young farmers out for a bit of fun after the pubs closed), hundreds of hedgehogs stamping around in circles in some synchronized mating ritual, the crushed corn imprints of the landing pads of extra-terrestrial space craft, the Earth itself, or friendly aliens or nature spirits trying to attract the human race's attention to encoded messages telling us – as if we didn't know already – that we were damaging the planet and threatening future generations' existence. And so on. There was indeed a tendency for many people to read into the circles their own belief system, to seek from them support for their model of the world. Which of course reminds us of the old adage – some people drink of the waters of the fountain of knowledge; others merely gargle.

In contrast, Colin Andrews, Pat Delgado, Terence Meaden and, later, the CCCS devoted themselves to gathering the evidence, trying to formulate a theory, and testing it by further observation or well-planned experiment. And going where the evidence led, even if they did not want to go. For unlike those people with cherished belief systems, who try to force the evidence to fit the Procrustean bed of their world model, the scientist (at least in principle) should follow evidence by theory and not the other way around.

As the years passed, members of the CCCS planned and carried out a wide variety of projects, striving to keep up with the increasing number and complexity of the formations, later called pictograms, that appeared. They designed and built various instruments to measure and record anomalies in magnetism, in the state of the crops within the circles, and reported effects on human beings. They set up cropwatches, where a particular area in which circles had appeared in previous years was secretly and continuously monitored to see if any circle would appear without human involvement. One early cropwatch I took part in was Operation White Crow, so named after Professor William James' statement that one sure way to disprove the theory that all crows are black, is to find one white crow. Therefore if one circle appeared with no human intervention, no-one could claim that all circles were man-made.

The era of Doug and Dave arrived, the two gentlemen who claimed to a delighted media that they had been creating the circles, sneaking out of their homes night-after-night, unbeknownst to their wives.

Most of us were quite prepared to take as a possibility that the simpler patterns of circles could have been made by the nocturnal duo or other pranksters, but we were more than doubtful if it was possible at night, even with ingenious equipment, to create in a few hours the precise and highly-complicated pictograms that were by now appearing, or to leave the corn, or wheat, or oilseed rape within the patterns in the states in which they were subsequently found. And so a renewed search was made for a litmus test to distinguish hoaxed formations (that is, man-made) from genuine formations. In the United States, Dr Levengood carried out a long series of examinations of samples sent to him from crop circles and from areas outside the circles, to try to establish any difference in the properties between circle cereal and control sample cereal.

By the mid-1990s, circle investigations were under attack on two fronts. On one there was the undoubted effort of various hoaxers, aided and abetted by a section of the press, to create as many hoaxed circles as possible. As part of this effort, some newspapers and some TV companies tried to trick investigators into visiting fakes and make unwise and premature judgements regarding their genuineness. On another front, the investigators, hampered by lack of money and numbers, were faced by the amused scepticism of the majority of scientists they tried to convince that in the crop circle phenomenon there was something worth taking seriously.

There are of course two types of sceptical reactions to any new and controversial phenomena. There are those sceptics who say immediately: 'These things cannot happen – therefore they don't.' Any seeming evidence must be fraudulent, or examples of faulty observations, or wishful thinking! Such people are quite often encountered by psychical researchers. They rarely have any track record in research in the field but they *know* what is possible and what is not possible. I call them 'Goldwyns', after the late Sam

Goldwyn who once memorably remarked: 'My mind is made up. Don't confuse me with facts.'

The other kind of sceptic has been called the pragmatic sceptic. Like a good scientist he keeps an open mind. He has not researched the phenomena himself, but when they are reported to him by someone for whom he has respect, he has to say something like this:

> It sounds interesting, though highly unlikely. It would need a lot of evidence to convince me. I would have to investigate it myself to be convinced and I agree that it should be investigated by the methods of science, but I am too busy with my own research projects, and in any case it is so controversial there is no money available to fund serious researches even if I wanted to do it.

The younger scientist might well add: 'I couldn't get involved in this. My department would object to me wasting my time in this fringe science and it would look bad on my record.'

The pragmatic sceptic is forced to remain outside the field (literally and figuratively!) but keeps an open mind.

Fair enough.

I myself am now outside the field but retain a keen interest in the crop circle phenomenon. I regret in no way the years I spent in the CCCS. The incredible beauty, complexity and circumstances in which many of the formations in recent years have appeared leave me unconvinced that they are all fakes. I have seen no demonstrations – even in daylight – that such formations can be produced precisely as they are in the available time or that the state of the crop within the circle or formation can be created. At the same time, I do not believe that many of these formations are of natural occurrence. They smack of intelligence. But if it is not of human origin, what is it? I simply do not know.

The phenomenon still continues. Are all the accounts given by Lucy Pringle in this book the result of lies, or wishful thinking, or gullibility? Those who have given such accounts comprise a wide distribution of intelligence and education. Their accounts are not sensationalized but sober yet puzzled in style. In the absence of any evidence to the contrary, I am prepared to accept that the vast majority of these people are telling the truth as they understand it.

This is why it is desirable that this book has been written. The proper study of the crop circle phenomenon still badly needs a truly scientific and sustained effort, and if this book helps to encourage that effort it will have been worthwhile. But in itself Lucy's book is well worth reading, and I for one am grateful that she has taken the trouble and patience to collate everything that she has learned in her years of observation and research. Someone once said that facts without a theory form a mob. Very true. But this mob, the formations in the fields and their associated phenomena, are beautiful, breathtaking and beguiling and still even now solicit an adequate explanation.

A.E. Roy
Professor Emeritus of Astronomy
University of Glasgow
Past-President, Centre for Crop Circle Studies

Contributors

I am deeply grateful to the many people who have contributed to this book. Without their help, enthusiasm and generosity, much of the material would never have come to light. I am particularly indebted to Keith Wakelam for his inspirational ideas, encouragement and wisdom, to Linda Daubney for drawing up the proposal and for her constant help and encouragement in making the impossible possible, and to Marion Simmonds for her enormous help in cross-referencing the illustrations, to Pat Delgado for allowing me the use of extracts from his newsletter, through which, in several cases, I was able to contact the original people involved, and to librarian Des Farnham and his staff at Petersfield Library.

Other principal contributors with whom I have spent many happy and productive hours in person or at a distance are:

Ray Barnes, Barbara Berge, Moona Beswick, Lesley Clementson, Diana Cussons, Chad Deetken, Bridget Engledow (deceased), Shirley Gifford, Gerald Hawkins, John Holman, John Houston, Shelley Keel, Janie Malone, Chris Mansell, Isabel Maxwell–Cade, Sarah Miles, James Millen, Karen and Michael Neary, Michael Newark, Roger Nicklin, Kobus Nieuwmeiser, Ralph Noyes (deceased), Margaret Randall, Barry Reynolds, Patricia Rhodes, David Russell, Ron Russell, A.J. Samuels, Roger Sear, Frederick Smith, Malcolm Stewart, Michael Strainic, Peter Staples, Nancy Talbot, Gary and Vivienne Tomlinson, André Tong, Paul Vigay, Kathy Wakelam (deceased), Christopher Weeks.

Photographers and Illustrators
Richard Andrews, Peter Baillie (deceased), Elizabeth Barnes, Julie and Stewart Ball, Charles Bone PPRI, ARCA, Hon FCA (Canada), Anthony Cheke, Leora Frankin, John Haddington, Michael Hubbard, Andrew King, David Kingston, Jürgen Kronig, Georgina Ling NDD, Terence Meaden, Debbie Pardoe, Dennis Pearson, Barry Reynolds, Russell Stannard, Nigel Tomsett, Grant Wakefield

My especial thanks also to Leora Franklin for her superb drawings and Nigel Tomsett and Debbie Pardoe for their magnificent drawn-to-scale silhouettes.

I am conscious that I may not have thanked everyone for their contributions to this book. Anyone I have omitted, please accept my very grateful thanks.

The Crop Circle Enigma

Virtually everyone has heard of crop circles, but what exactly are they? How are they made, and (perhaps more importantly), why and by whom? This book attempts to answer some of these questions, by gathering together many ordinary people's accounts of their experiences of crop circles – both how they felt while in them and afterwards, the effects the circles can have on animals and machinery, and a few reactions of eyewitnesses to the beauty of these strange phenomena.

The most striking features of these markings in crops are the neat swirling and flattening of the crop, and the sharp cut-off point between the flattened crop and the rest of the standing crop. Do the formations always appear circular? Certainly not! They are becoming more and more elaborate as time goes on, and now consist of extremely complex geometric patterns with many different elements – as the briefest of glances at the illustrations in this book will show.

Do the formations only appear in cereal crops? Again – no. Crop formations have appeared in fields of potatoes, vegetables, sugar cane, sunflowers, grass, thistles and heather, in rice paddies, snow, ice and sand, and even in fruit orchards.

Crop circles have been turning up all over the world. There are eyewitness reports of circles in Russia, Japan, America, Canada, Australia, New Zealand, Bulgaria, France, Spain, Germany, South Africa and Israel – to name just a few. The numbers do seem concentrated in the UK, with around 2,000 reported circles (although this may be due to more people looking out for them than elsewhere – as they are often located in remote, hard-to-find places, best spotted from the air). However, the Netherlands have had 97 reported cases, America 50, and Japan and Germany over 30 cases each.

One very common misconception is that crop circles are a recent phenomenon. However, as time goes

Figure 1: Woodcut of 'The Mowing Devil'

on there are more and more reports of circles having been seen prior to the 1980s and 1990s. I have been sent reports of circles appearing in Ireland in the 1930s, and other reports (not just from this part of the world but from as far afield as South Africa) from the 1940s right through to the 1970s. The earliest representation of a crop circle occurs in a woodcut of 1687, which depicts the famous 'Mowing Devil' reaping a field of oats into a flattened circle.

Apparently the farmer refused to pay the amount asked by a particular reaper, muttering that 'he would rather the Devil took his oats'. During the night strange sounds and lights were heard and seen, and the following morning the farmer found part of his crop lying in round circles – whereupon he promptly fled.

More recently, there are many reports from people who remember playing among circles when they were children back in the 1930s, 1940s and 1950s, and some even in the 1920s. One of the things these stories have in common is that the circles were regarded as nothing unusual – Moona Beswick remembers playing in crop circles as a child near Ware in Hertfordshire: 'They've always been around and no one used to think there was anything strange about them. They were great fun to play in, although the farmers weren't so pleased!' John Houston remembers playing in wheat circles in 1943 and 1944 while an evacuee in Rowd, Wiltshire. 'They had completely neat edges, and the wheat on the bottom was laid smoothly, all going in the same direction forming a curved parallel to the outside circle.' They were looked upon as 'things that just happened' by the locals; 'things that only came one at a time and only when terrible times were about'. This was, of course, the 'terrible time' of the war.

Some of the earliest present-day eyewitness reports date from the 1930s. A Mrs Songhurst saw crop circles 60 years ago while living in Ireland, in Co. Donegal. The circles were large and all swirled anti-clockwise. The people would have had no reason to fake such circles, in fact quite the opposite: their survival depended on the price they could obtain for their grain, and any reports indicating something was amiss with their crops would have been disaster. The farmers even attempted to stand the corn up again!

One Sussex woman remembers playing in corn formations during the war, like John Houston.

Figure 2: An Iron Age hillfort

'The thing that surprises me about the circles in the corn is the suggestion that they are recent. I can remember them with absolute clarity 50 years ago when I was a small child and my friends and I spent hours playing in them. There were two fields in particular where they occurred regularly over three or four years. There were two or three circles in the fields and they were all swirled round flat and had well-defined edges. There was an interconnecting pathway between the circles which was not straight but curved. It was only one or two inches wide with the stems splayed sideways. We pretended the circles were made by German parachutists...The grown-ups never took any notice of the circles, having more pressing business, and it would never occur to anyone to take photos or involve the media.'

This phlegmatic response is echoed today by many local rural people: David Russell (a renowned dowser) fell into conversation one summer's day in Pewsey, Wiltshire with an 80 year-old, who had lived in the village all his life, as had his family before him. The topic of crop circles came up, and the old man expressed surprise at all the 'fuss': he had been brought up with circles – they had always been there, and he couldn't understand the sudden interest! It seems to me quite possible that crop circles have been appearing since the dawn of time, although perhaps not in their present, elaborate form. They certainly do seem to be linked to hill carvings (such as the chalk horse at Uffington), ancient monuments (like Stonehenge and the great stone circle at Avebury), and the many, many prehistoric barrows and sacred places which occur, for example, round Wessex.

Were our Neolithic ancestors the first witnesses of crop formations? It is surely not outside the realms of possibility that they tried to commemorate and record these unusual happenings with stones and rocks. Maybe places like Stonehenge originated as a visible record of a crop circle, who knows?

The biggest question is, of course, how are the circles made? Are they miracles or works of the Devil? Are they all man-made, or is there an unknown intelligence working behind the scenes? Could they be made by atmospheric conditions, such as plasma vortices, or natural energy lines? Could they be the

Figure 3: © Elizabeth Barnes

result of whirling dervishes, rutting hedgehogs, alien spacecraft, or even maids with chamber-pots?

Some investigators have subscribed to the following hypothesis concerning the formation of a crop circle. Whatever 'force' it is that causes circles to form, hits the ground vertically, creating a huge electrical discharge at the point of impact (rather like the effect of ball lightning hitting the ground). This results in microwave activity which softens the base of the corn stalks, allowing them to fall over but not break – unlike hoaxed formations, genuine circles do not contain plants with crushed stems. The electrical discharge then travels up the interior of the plants and, when the force gets too great, escapes through 'explosion cavities' in the stem joints. This is similar to the effect of putting a jacket potato in a microwave oven without first pricking it: the potato will explode. Again, these little 'explosion cavities' are clearly visible in genuine crop circles, but are sadly missing from the man-made ones.

The vast majority of crop circles in this country occur on the chalk lands of the Wessex triangle. Under the chalk lie aquifers (underground water sources), which almost certainly accounts for the high incidence of formations in this part of the country, as water attracts electricity. There are also many 'energy' or geodetic stress lines here. These lines move in harmony with the Earth's tectonic plates, and release electromagnetic fields when they shift. All genuine crop formations appear on these energy lines.

The fact that the formations simultaneously represent perfect aspects of many disciplines from mathematics and geometry, through engineering and music, to astrological and astronomical symbols lends credence to the suggestion of the involvement of some external, unknown intelligence. The 'Julia Set', which appeared in 1996 in a field opposite the site of Stonehenge, is one such example. To the mathematicians and geometers it is a representation of the computer-generated fractal image, the Julia set; to a musician it is a base clef; to a marine biologist, a perfect example of the cross-section of a nautillus and, finally, to the medical fraternity it constitutes a mammalian skeleton with precisely the correct number of vertebrae. Alternatively, the formations could be manifestations of our own subconscious.

This book recounts just some of the hundreds of reports that I have come across. I haven't attempted to look for any answers, but merely to record what ordinary, sane people know to be the facts.

Lucy Pringle
1998

Figure 4: The 'Julia Set' and Stonehenge, Wiltshire, 7 July 1996. 919 ft x 508 ft (278 m x 154 m), 151 circles. Wheat

Chapter One

Eyewitness Reports

Many people who have witnessed a crop circle forming are often reluctant to come forward and speak
about it, either because they do not quite believe
what they have seen, or for fear of ridicule. However,
as the phenomenon becomes more widely accepted
and discussed, reports are trickling in. This chapter
contains just a few of these eyewitness reports of
crop circles' forming.

IT ALL HAPPENED SO QUICKLY

Gary and Vivienne Tomlinson witnessed a circle
forming at Hambledon, Surrey in 1990. Thursday 17
May was a warm, sticky and unusually still day. In
the evening, around 8 p.m., Gary and Vivienne
decided to go for a walk across the fields to Bryony
Hill, a local landmark.

Figure 5: Gary and Vivienne Tomlinson looking towards
Bryony Hill.

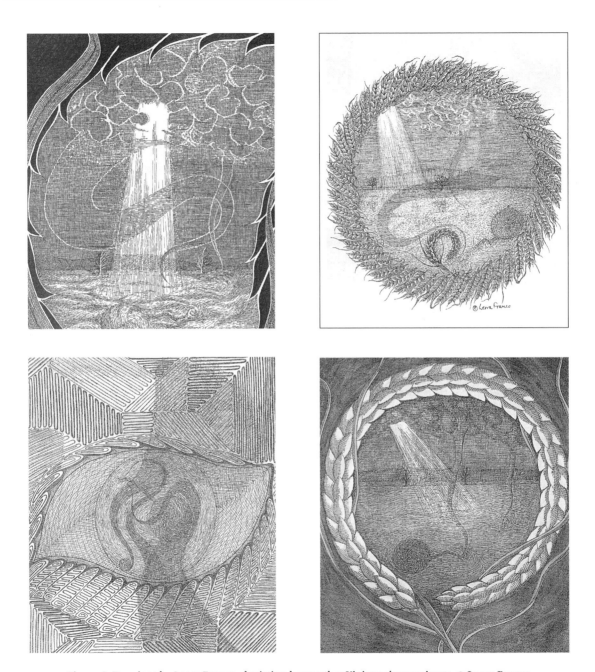

Figure 6: Drawings by Leora Franco, depicting her mother Vivienne's experience. © Leora Franco

'The air hung heavy and still as we made our way along the public footpath beside the field; the corn was light green in colour and stood about two feet high. As we walked along we noticed two very small and perfectly formed circles: one by the edge of the crop, one slightly further in. We thought nothing of them until later. We walked up Bryony Hill and remarked as we went along that the air was heavy, humid and still, and we quickly got out of breath climbing the steep hill. At last we reached the top of Hydon's Ball (as the peak is known), where we sat for a while and enjoyed the scenery.

'Eventually, we decided to walk back down the hill as the sun was setting and we hadn't brought torches. We were crossing the second of the wheat fields when the wind began. Until then it had been quite still. We were standing about 100 metres from Hydon's Ball. The sky was fairly overcast but ahead of us a touch of blue could be seen through a spectacular sunset, which threw a golden glow over the cornfield. There was so much light on the corn it had a mirror-like appearance.

'It was at this stage that we noticed the wind blowing the corn, sending wave after wave of ripples across the crop on our right, making it appear like a golden-brown sea. The wind towards Bryony Hill was strong. The trees were leaning over on their sides and below in the cornfield the wind continued.

'Suddenly, in a matter of seconds, a band of mist rolled across and down from the top of the hill. It all happened so quickly. The wind pattern changed – the band of mist seemed to come between two trees at the end of the field; continuing on, it appeared to be pushing from two directions *and* surging forwards. At the centre of the mist the wind gathered force, sending strong waves as it went. The whirlwind seemed to appear at this point. It looked like a mist or light fog, and was shimmering.

'We could hear the noise of the wind. The whistling grew stronger as the wind intensified and reached a high pitch like a set of Pan-pipes, ending on one continuous note. The noise was tremendous. The corn was being pushed down as the spinning air made its way towards us. We both looked up to see if there was a helicopter above.

'Suddenly, there was a strong gust of wind pushing us from the side and from above. The shimmering air circled around us. It was forcing down hard on our heads. We could hardly stand upright, yet we felt as if we were being sucked up at the same time. There was tremendous pressure from both above and below. We felt tingly all over, like pins and needles from head to foot. Our hair was standing on end.

'All at once the wind scooped us off the path into the cornfield. We took a great buffeting. It was very frightening. Looking down we saw a circle being formed around us. It only took a couple of seconds. A spiral appeared anti-clockwise and grew outwards from the centre, about two metres in diameter.

'In the centre of the circle there was a small pyramid of corn, the stalks stacked up against each other. The whirlwind split in two, one part going into the distance, skimming over the top of the corn as it went. The second part whizzed past to one side, pushing down the corn and then forming a second circle a little further away. Again, this only took a few seconds. We looked around for the first whirlwind and could still see it, like a light shimmering mist, as it zig-zagged into the distance over the top of the corn.

'Interesting things were happening in the circle in which we were standing. Miniature whirlwinds were appearing one after the other; small,

glistening vortices perhaps four inches [10cms] apart. They whirled around the corn in small bunches towards the perimeter, gently laying the corn down and enlarging the circle. The wind had dropped completely and it seemed strange watching these shimmering whirlwinds as they spun around.

'We both turned towards the second whirlwind, which looked like a transparent glowing tube stretching endlessly into the sky. The light was beginning to fade. By now, the miniature whirlwinds seemed to have lost their misty look, appearing more like watery glass with a quivering line inside. They wobbled slowly, still running

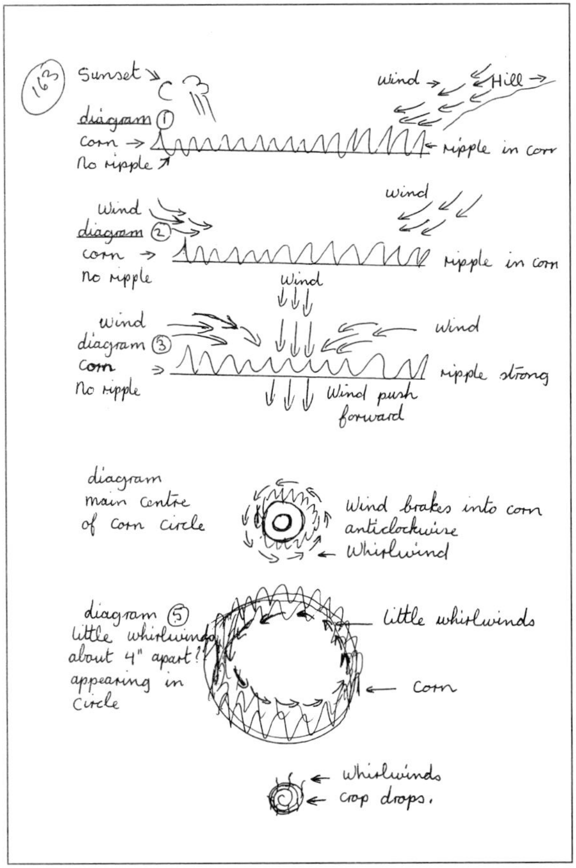

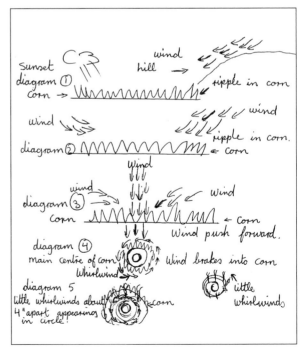

Figure 7a and b: Vivienne's recollections of the events. © Vivienne Tomlinson

Figure 7b

along the wall of the circle. There also seemed to be fewer of them.

'It was growing dark, and slowly we made our way back home in silence, stunned by the event. We both felt lethargic and nauseous, and were suffering from shock.'

Neither Gary nor Vivienne were wearing watches at the time. They estimate the duration of the episode to have been approximately seven minutes, but it seemed to last an eternity. Vivienne's ears were so painful, she went to see her doctor who diagnosed perforated ear drums. She had never had any previous trouble with her ears. For both of them, the lethargy and nausea took about a week to wear off. They also suffered from 'heavy and tired' eyes.

Physically, Gary and Vivienne have recovered from their ordeal; psychologically the effect is more long term. They are unable to talk to anyone else who would understand what they have been through – for although other people have seen circles appear, they have not actually experienced one forming around them – and consequently feel very isolated.

IT ONLY TOOK FOUR SECONDS

Ray Barnes is a dedicated researcher and observer of nature. He has witnessed and experienced more strange happenings than most people would in several lifetimes. One such event took place in Westbury, Wiltshire, in 1981.

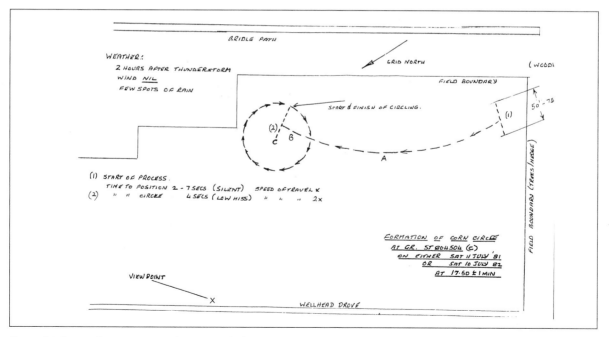

Figure 8: Diagram by Ray Barnes of a crop circle forming. © Ray Barnes

During the evening of Saturday 11 July, Ray witnessed a crop circle form. He was taking his dog for a walk after a thunderstorm earlier that afternoon; in fact it was still raining slightly.

'My attention was first drawn to a wave or line coming through the top of the cereal crop [at position 1, see Figure 8]. After travelling across the field at an arc, the "line" dropped to the ground [at position 2], and radially described a circle in a clockwise direction in approximately four seconds.

'There are several points to make about the line. To begin with, it was invisible, just a wave cutting through the corn. In addition, there was absolutely no wind, and the line exhibited no fluid tendencies – that is, its speed was constant and there were no wind waves before or after it. The line just appeared, and there was no disturbance of hedge or trees at the field boundary. The estimated speed of the line was about 50 mph [80 kph], and there was no visual aberration in front, above or behind it. The line almost disappeared where the ground dips [between points A and B on Figure 8], so it would seem it was maintaining a constant height irrespective of ground contour.

'The crop heads only "jiggled", rather than being bent, which would seem to indicate that the line had holes in it like the teeth of a giant comb, or that the line was sufficiently weak for the cereal heads to pop through it when the pressure of them reached a certain level. The circle itself was described radially (not diametrically), and at a constant speed, and was executed in a single sweep. If there were other sweeps, I didn't see them. The peripheral speed of the circle seemed to be about twice that of the line arc speed.

'The crop in the circle went down as neatly as if it had been cut by a giant flan cutter. There was absolutely no spring back, which was rather awe inspiring; if, for instance, you watch a tractor crossing a field there is always some springing back of the flattened crop.'

WHO WERE THOSE MEN?

André Tong was born in Boughton, a little village in Kent where his family has lived for many generations. He is a farmer specializing in fruit-tree grafting. One day in September, 1979, André was inspecting some apple trees to see if the fruit was ready for picking.

'I had bought the trees from a farmer at a fruit auction, because he didn't want to have the trouble of picking the crop. On this particular morning, I noticed a lot of fruit was missing in the middle of the orchard and the leaves had been stripped from the branches – except from the very tips of the slender branches. The grass mowings had also been sucked away.

'At first I thought it might have been children, but it was such a large area it would have taken them a week to have done so much damage. It couldn't have been the weather, because there was no fruit on the ground – everything had been sucked away. The conditions were very warm and there was no wind. It must have happened the previous night because the day before everything was alright.

'When I looked more closely, I could see that the area that was bare was a complete circle. With those trees on the edge of the circle, half the tree was alright, the other was stripped bare of fruit. It was a large area of about one acre.

'As I examined the damage at about 9 a.m., I noticed three people, all the same size, walking between the trees. They were dressed in what looked like grey shell-suits.

'I approached them and called out "What are you doing?", thinking they must have had something to do with the missing crop. I got to within 20–30 feet [6–9m] of them, but they didn't turn round, so I assumed that they hadn't heard me. I walked a bit faster and as I got closer I felt I could not breathe. I felt a pressure as though I had been stopped by an invisible wall. It was pushing me back as though I was trying to move in a dream, but couldn't. Then the people just faded away.

'I looked at my watch and found that it was lunch time. I could not account for those three lost hours.

'I was very worried about the incident. The apple loss was around £4,000 and the fruit had not been insured because of the high cost involved. I called on a friend in the local police force and together we inspected the damage, but could throw no light on the occurrence.

'My friend didn't make out a report, as he had no more ideas than I had and we agreed to keep quiet about it for the fear of ridicule. I never told my friend about the strange people, again for fear of local ridicule.

'If you have lived on the land all your life, 90 per cent of things can be explained; it's the other 10 per cent for which there is no explanation.'

André had previously served as a bomb disposal expert in Ireland, where he also lived on and off for 15 years until he was involved in an accident while defusing a bomb.

Not only has André been trained to have a highly logical, analytical and critical mind but he is also a true countryman, born a man of the soil, and, having lived on the land most of his life, he notices things others would miss, for the seasons and all their changes play an important role in his life.

An interesting footnote to this story is that for 24 hours after this experience, André clearly remembers that everything he ate or drank tasted of almonds. He also developed red itchy blotches on his skin, for which no medical explanation was ever found.

The orchard is now a field and while dowsing there I found an energy line running directly through it to a field, about three miles away, from which a crop of sprouts also disappeared (*see below*).

SOME OF OUR VEGETABLES ARE MISSING

This story, of a winter-crop circle, is a timely reminder not to allow our minds to become set in any rigid, fixed patterns. We tend to 'assume' that crop circles are a summer phenomenon and that all circles appear in cereal crops. This is demonstrably not the case.

One morning in December 1978, André Tong noticed that some of his sprouts were missing from the corner of his field.

'We went over to have a look. There was a very well-defined circle with a large area. All the sprouts were laying flat to the ground and appeared to have been gently pushed into that position. None of the sprouts were broken at the base, and they were laying in an anti-clockwise direction. There was a dead pheasant on top of the sprouts. It might only have been dead for a few hours because it was still pliable.

'How the incident happened is very strange; the ground was very hard due to the frosty weather, none of the sprouts were broken and there was no frost on the sprouts or the pheasant in the circle.'

This would seem to indicate some change in temperature inside the circle as distinct from the area outside it. Another point worth mentioning is the fragility of the sprout stalks. Being hollow stemmed, they would normally be extremely brittle and break with some ease. However, this was not the case – none of the stalks were broken.

The sprouts were not the only vegetables to disappear without trace. In January 1997, near Canterbury, Kent, André and his men were pruning apple trees when they noticed that in the field next to them there were some large holes in the cabbage field.

'We went over to have a look and found there were three circles: one large and two smaller ones. In all the circles the cabbages had gone. I went and told the farmer in case he might have thought my men had taken them.

'When we went back to the field we noticed all the stones, large and small, had been sucked out.

It must have happened very slowly because the soil hadn't been disturbed. The weather conditions were very light rain. There were six holes about four inches [10cms] across in the large circle – we don't know how deep they were. These holes were quite smooth inside, as though a pole had gone in. We dropped a four-foot [1.2m] stick into one hole and it just vanished.'

André's final account takes place at Castlebellingham, in Co. Louth, Ireland, in October 1987. The farmer called André to look at one of his fields – a field of carrots.

'A large, clear, star-like impression had been taken out of the field. It was shaped like a circle with a four-pointed star; the side points were half the size of the end points. The carrots had just been sucked out of the ground. There was nothing left, not a single carrot, not even holes where the carrots had been – and the carrots in Ireland are the size of a man's fist.

'There are rarely frosts in that part of Ireland and the carrots had been left in the ground in order to produce a better crop. The farmer was very cross that "someone" had taken his carrots, and it was particularly strange as people in Ireland don't mess about damaging fields.

'The field was about four Irish acres (which are slightly larger than English acres), and the star shape from which the carrots had disappeared was about one acre – the farmer measured it out with his stick. It would have taken a lot of people to dig up that amount of carrots!

'We looked for tracks but none were found;

Figure 9: Circle in a potato field, Market Rasen, 1990.
© John Howard

there was no apparent explanation and I didn't want to tell the farmer what I really thought. He wouldn't have believed me.

'Afterwards, I thought about it – the amount of people you would have needed to dig up the carrots; all the lights you would have to use, bearing in mind it was night; arc lights, which the farmer would have seen – you would have needed a hundred people and many trucks to do all that.'

Potato fields have also been affected. During the summer of 1990 John Howard, a photographer from Market Rasen in Leicestershire, was called to take a picture of a curious circle which had appeared overnight in a potato field. The circle was approximately nine yards (8m) in diameter and was actually a broad ellipse rather than a circle.

Within the ellipse, all the plants were flattened and destroyed, with dead leaves and stems; in the rest of the field the crop was strong and healthy, standing one or two feet high. There was a sharp cut-off point between the flattened potatoes and the standing crop, and there were no signs of entry or exit marks leading to or from the ellipse; nor were there any marks on the soil. As the rest of the crop was quite healthy, disease and poor soil quality were ruled out as causes. A second, less regular circle appeared in a neighbouring field of potatoes about the same time. The only out-of-the-ordinary recent occurrence was that there had been a thunderstorm that night.

TALES FROM THE TURNIP FIELDS

As we have seen, crop formations are not just a summer phenomenon. In November 1991 I went up to Cheesefoot Head in Hampshire to see if there was any evidence of secondary growth appearing where circles had occurred during the summer. I drove down a hill towards where a formation (the 'Tree of Life') (Figure 10a) had been in barley, close to the junction with the Winchester road. Passing field after field of freshly ploughed earth, I suddenly saw a replica of the 'Tree of Life' in a crop of fodder turnips, in exactly the same place it had appeared that summer (Figure10b).

According to the farm manager, the turnips had been planted in September, after the barley had been reaped. The ground had been thoroughly ploughed and turned – the field was disced twice to a depth of four inches (10cms) maximum before the turnips were planted, 'thereby moving every part of the ground'.

Figure 10a: 'Tree of Life' in barley. July 1991. West of Gypsy Lane, Cheesefoot Head, Hampshire. 71½ ft (22m) at its widest point. © Jürgen Kronig

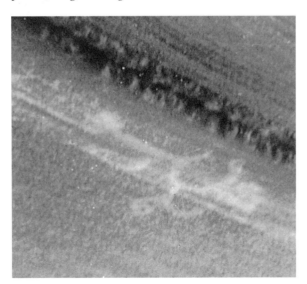

Figure 10b: 'Tree of Life' in a field of turnips. November 1991. West of Gypsy Lane, Cheesefoot Head, Hampshire. 71½ ft (22m) at its widest point

I THEN PASSED OUT

Frederick Smith, who now lives in New South Wales, Australia, recalls the formation of a quintuplet of circles as far back as 1947, when he was working on a farm in the Lincolnshire fenland. Incidently, this is the earliest report of a quintuplet formation prior to the 1980s.

'I was 18 years old at the time. The month was April and the weather was very good, just nice and a gentle breeze with no planes in the air at the time.'

Frederick recalls that as the circles were laid down, there was a noise 'like a gentle hum or buzz, i.e., a few bees. When the circles were laid down the noise was

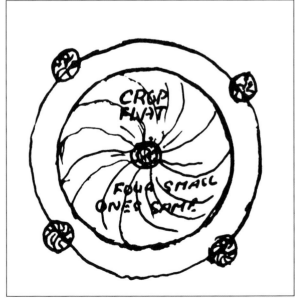

Figure 11: Diagram of the lay of the crop. © Frederick Smith

Figure 12: Silbury Hill and the 'Beltane Wheel'. Oil seed rape. Ringed circle with standing crop in the centre and 33 scrolls accurately fitted into the ring. *c.*250–280 ft (76–85m) diameter. Formed between 3 and 5 a.m.

a high-pitched buzz which seemed to come from far away.' The circles took approximately three minutes to form. While this was happening, 'I first felt faint, and then passed out.'

Frederick came round after about three hours, just as the crop (which was green oats, six or seven inches high (*c.*15cms) and not yet in seed) was beginning to stand up again, after sustaining no damage at all. The fact that Frederick passed out for such a length of time seems to indicate that there may have been a

rapid loss of air pressure around him. This sort of air pressure drop occurs when an aircraft dives steeply, necessitating the use of oxygen masks.

HE HEARD NOTHING UNUSUAL

This is an account from more recent times.

Early on the evening of Sunday 3 May 1998 a young Scot, who wanted to video the moon rising

Figure 13: Beltane Wheel design on a mosaic from Fishbourne Roman palace

the oil seed rape crop in the adjacent field. This formation consisted of 33 geometrically perfect scrolls lying within an outer ring – strikingly similar in appearance to a mosaic in the Roman Palace of Fishbourne, Chichester, and also to the Celtic Beltane Wheel.

Although two hours seems fast for the creation of a complex formation of such large proportions, it is by no means unusual.

Early in July 1996 a pilot flew a light aircraft over the field opposite Stonehenge at 5.50 p.m., on his way from Exeter to Thruxton, and saw nothing in the field. Half-an-hour later, a second pilot spotted the enormous and spectacular Julia Set in the previously empty field, measuring some 915 feet by 508 feet (277m by 154m) in the wheat. A gamekeeper and a security guard at the monument both confirm that the formation was not there in the morning, but had appeared by the evening, and there is evidence from the police that the pictogram formed in under 15 minutes

over West Kennett Long Barrow, near Silbury Hill, took up position in a field called The Sanctuary.

He fell asleep around 3 a.m. on the Monday morning, having neither seen nor heard anything unusual. He woke at 5 a.m. to find a massive formation, in excess of 250 feet (76m) in diameter, deeply etched in

Chapter Two

The Great Crop Circle Hoax?

Although reports of crop circles have been circulating for many, many years, occurring in many different countries, the recent upsurge in the phenomenon has brought with it the inevitable hoaxers, no doubt encouraged by sensationalized media reports, reports which at times verge on a deliberate campaign of disinformation. This has to beg the question, 'Why?'

THE FIRST HOAXING REVELATIONS

The end of the summer of 1991 saw the 'Doug and Dave' revelations. Doug Bower and Dave Chorley, two Southampton sexagenarians (according to the newspapers), had been making crop circle formations for the previous ten years right under our noses, and also, for that matter, under the unsuspecting noses of their spouses, who seemed to be blissfully unaware of the nocturnal escapades of their loved ones!

The timing of these exposés was brilliant for the tabloid newspapers, boosting flagging sales and creating great excitement all over the world. However, whereas the Doug and Dave story had been expertly timed, so (unintentionally), had the publication of the preliminary results of scientific tests performed by two American crop circle researchers, Marshall Dudley (an electronic and nuclear consultant of Tennessee) and Dr Levengood (a biophysicist of Pinelandia Biophysics Laboratory, Michigan).

These tests revealed that we were on the way to being able to distinguish once and for all between the real and hoaxed article. There was clear evidence that certain of the formations tested could not have been made by man. Reports of these findings were sent to the national papers, but such was the success of the hoaxing story in raising newspaper sales that these reports, which would have debunked the hoaxers' claims, were never printed and to this day languish in some dusty files. Obviously, good news doesn't sell copy!

DISINFORMATION INFORMATION

Early in 1998, three crop circle hoaxers, whom here I shall call Wynken, Blynken and Nod (with apologies to Eugene Field (1850–1895)), were paid considerable sums by National Broadcasting Corporation (NBC) television to make a crop circle in New Zealand. No expense was spared, all their costs were met. Certain criteria were apparently laid down, such as the number of elements to be included in the formation, the

Figure 14: Filming with the BBC *Country File* team, August 1997

length of time allowed to make it, and that it should be done in total darkness.

Armed with 'flattening' equipment and diagrams drawn to scale, they were flown to Dunearn in Central Southland, many miles from the eyes and ears of any 'croppie' authorities. The shoot went ahead and the formation was made. Unfortunately for them, local people reported cranes being brought into the place and floodlights trained on the field where the hoaxers were working, giving them the benefit of seeing exactly what they were doing.

To give the hoaxers credit, the finished result looked impressive from the air. However, ground photographs of the lay of the flattened crop were briefly shown on the Internet. These photos showed a mess of broken and crushed stems (unlike the genuine article), and were so revealing of the deception that they were quickly taken off, never to be shown again. In contrast, NBC programmes covering the event and showing the aerial shots have been given prime viewing time in both the United States and Canada.

DISINFORMATION (CONTINUED)

In the summer of 1997 I was approached by the BBC's *Country File* programme to do a piece on crop formations to catch up on the scientific research and findings, as they had not covered the subject for several years.

Most of the programme was shot in the famous 1997 Double Fractal formation below the Milk Hill White Horse at Alton Barnes, Wiltshire.

As filming progressed, it became obvious that the

producers were not really interested in the scientific findings at all; they were far more interested in the views of people casually visiting the formation (such as one man with his two small daughters who, when interviewed, said they believed the formations were made by 'little green men'!), rather than my research on the effects of electromagnetic fields on living matter, and other scientific findings. In fact, at the end of the first day, they had still not asked me any questions about this research.

The next morning I was asked to meet the *Country File* team at Teaglese Down, East Meon, in Hampshire where they took me into a formation and questioned me about its authenticity. Knowing how other crop circle investigators had been lured into making unfortunate statements, prominently presented and preserved forever on film, I was forewarned. On examining the fallen crop I found crushed stalks, seedheads knocked off and seeds strewn on the ground beneath the fallen crop. Clearly either I was not the first person into this formation or else it was man-made. I indicated this, much to the discomfort of the team. It turned out to have been made that morning by Doug Bower, the same Doug Bower who, together with Dave Chorley, claimed that they had made all the circles since circledom began!

As we were leaving the field, one of the producers proudly showed me part of the formation he had made personally. He seemed very pleased with himself and had clearly enjoyed the exercise. 'Did we have another budding hoaxer in our midst?', I asked myself.

When the programme was shown in the autumn, little green men and Doug Bower featured prominently. But where were the scientific findings?

MORE MURKY DEALINGS

In July 1998 the *Country File* team were back in Wiltshire, interviewing 'believers', i.e. people who treat formation occurrences more as a religion, rather than as a rational, scientific phenomenon.

The team had decided to do a piece on that great 'character', Doug Bower. Various other hoaxers had also turned up – a veritable hoaxers' convention! Rumour had it that, as Doug was not such an adept at circles (he can only make simple formations), *Country File* were going to commission the other, more artistically advanced group of Wynken, Blynken and Nod to make a complex formation, plonk the evergreen Bower in the centre and film him as being the generator of the masterpiece, thereby implying to the general public that all formations were man-made.

Yet, if this *were* so, who made the earliest crop circle reported, in 1687, and why do they still keep appearing on the same night all over the world in many different crops, and in no crops at all – in ice, snow, heather, sand and tree tops too? Doug, Wynken, Blynken and Nod must not only have solved the problem of immortality, but also the knotty puzzle of time and space travel too!

On the night of Saturday 26 July, the BBC team were discovered, by chance, actually recording two formations being made. These were being filmed from ground level using infra-red film. Despite the hoaxers' claims that they have made hundreds of circles since 1976, this was the first time anyone had been caught in the act.

The larger, complex formation was being made by Wynken, Blynken and Nod; the simple circle by

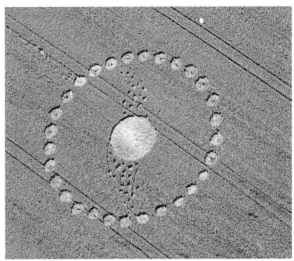

Figure 15: The two formations made for the BBC at Milk Hill. Doug Bower's circle is on the left

Figure 16: 'Daisy Chain', Cheriton, near Winchester, Hampshire, 6 July 1997. Barley

Bower and the very same BBC producer who had first tried out his skills at East Meon the previous year! As the nights are comparatively short at that time of summer, they were working in daylight for most of the time. However, Bower and friend still failed to complete their circle in the time and had to be helped by the others.

Immediately after they had finished, Wynken, Blynken and Nod were challenged about the sorry state of the lay of the crop and the thick 'tracer' rings of fallen crop clearly linking the circles. They replied that they always used the same construction method and it was not their fault if it looked messy, it must be due to the characteristics of that particular crop! What a contrast between their miserable efforts and the simple but beautiful Daisy Chain that appeared at Cheriton, Hampshire in 1997; each circle (containing standing stems of barley) is clearly separate from its

neighbour, showing no connecting line at all.

HOW TO SPOT THE HOAXES

Genuine formations contain certain elements that hoaxers are unable to replicate, such as the unbroken stalks (oil seed rape stalks are particularly fragile, due to their hollow nature, and snap if they are bent at more than 40 degrees; in genuine crop circles, however, they can be laid down at 90 degrees, and remain undamaged) and 'explosion cavities' already mentioned in the Introduction. Man-made formations all have weight applied in some degree to the crop, leading to broken and damaged plants. The seeds are not knocked out of the seedheads in a genuine formation, and the plants seem to continue to grow as usual.

One Wiltshire farmer gave permission for a man-made circle to be created on his land. Once it was completed, he was amazed that it very quickly attracted a mass of birds. Some years earlier, a crop circle had appeared on his land that the birds did not visit. The answer, as he found after a quick look at his 'new' circle, was that when the hoaxers had flattened the crop, they had knocked the seeds out of the seed-heads and provided a feast for all the local wildlife.

As mentioned above, in genuine formations the crop is not damaged in any physically visible way. In the immature crop a grey film is present, which occurs naturally and is part of the growing process of arable plants. If any weight is applied, or if you rub against the crop, this film is removed, never to be replaced. So, if you have the privilege of entering an immature crop circle and observe this grey film intact, not just at surface level but right through all the levels down to the ground, you have every right to be excited over the prospect of being in a genuine formation.

Although both immature and mature crop circles seem to continue to grow as normal, when the 'force' hits the crop in its immature (green) stage, before the seeds have developed, a condition called poly-embrony often occurs, in which no seeds develop. Conversely, when the 'force' hits the mature plant, the seeds become wizened and dehydrated. Repeated tests have shown that, not only do these seeds germinate more quickly than control seeds, but, illogically, they also need less water.

It is generally accepted by mathematicians that genuine formations contain sacred or Euclidian geometry, using the vital numbers of 5, 6 and 7. The *Country File* formation, despite looking as impressive from the air as the team's New Zealand effort, contained nine-fold geometry (see Figure 17), giving an angle of 40 degrees, which has no relationship to any of the numbers of importance or interest (such as the Golden Ratio), and several mathematical errors.

In contrast, the complex 1998 Clanfield formation, near Petersfield (Figure 18), is a mathematical event containing faultlessly exact and specific principles.

WHY ALL THE FUSS AND NONSENSE?

What is the purpose of all these programmes? Why are the media intent on spreading this disinformation? Of what are they scared?

It seems that hoaxing must continue in a self-perpetuating cycle for, as suggested by Paul Vigay:

Hoaxers MUST be able to prove that ALL formations are hoaxes, for it is they that claim the subject to be a hoax. All hoaxers have to do is to stop hoaxing. That way there would be no more circles. The biggest problem for the hoaxers is that of the genuine phenomenon. As they have no control over the 'real' circles, they cannot force the phenomenon to stop merely because they stop. Therefore each year, as genuine formations start to appear, the hoaxers have to come forward and say 'yes, we did them'. They cannot simply give up hoaxing as this will reveal the genuine formations, which will continue to appear. Hoaxers have effectively given themselves no option but to continue hoaxing for as long as the genuine phenomenon persists. The task becomes increasingly more difficult every year, as more and more 'crop watchers' monitor fields during the season. The hoaxers

Figure 17: The hoax formation at Milk Hill, with a diagram revealing 'bad' geometry.
© Ian Baillie

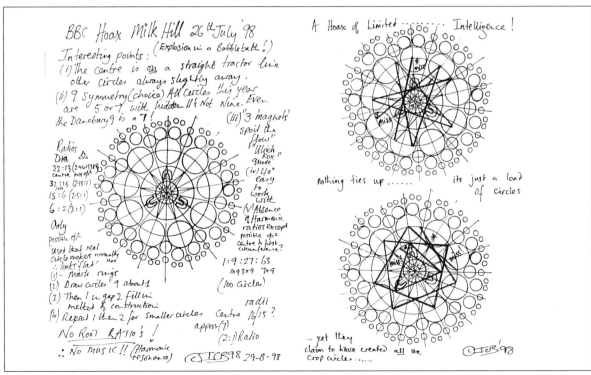

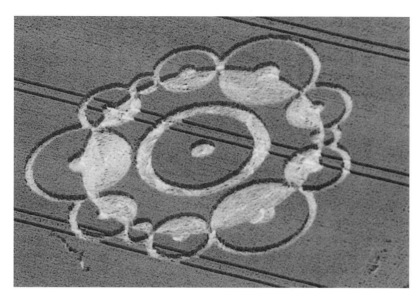

Figure 18: The formation at Clanfield in Hampshire, June 1998, showing elegant, correct geometry.
© Ian Baillie

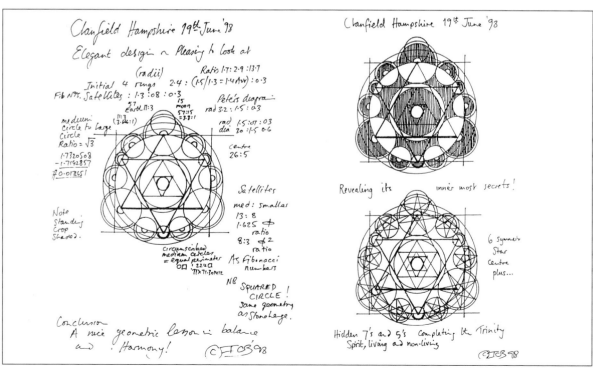

will therefore have to travel further and further to find a field not being watched. Eventually the hoaxers will either have to give an enormous amount of effort for nothing (or personal satisfaction) or simply give up.

Crop Circle Hoaxing: Is it a threat to the genuine phenomenon?

A report by Paul Vigay, 1994

One of the most bizarre anomalies of the crop circle phenomenon is the 'U turn' syndrome. The reason it is so striking is because it seems to affect researchers who, up until that time, had been among the most dedicated and open-minded. The first symptom is the 'wobble', in which they start reacting to the phenomenon in an uncharacteristic, inconsistent manner. This initially can be dismissed as the result of a late night, or some other minor physical disorder. The next stage becomes apparent when these inconsistencies can no longer be explained away rationally and it becomes hard to hold a sensible and logical discussion with the individual.

Stories about visits from men in grey suits are alluded to in hushed undertones. This, according to some, is the turning point, from which time on the recipients of these visits are 'never the same since'.

The final stage is reached when the individual needs to proclaim publicly that there is no longer a phenomenon, that he can prove without doubt that all, or nearly all, formations are man-made. He cannot see that if even one formation is genuine his argument is lost. He has a mission to impart. He is now as obsessed by the need to discredit the phenomenon as he was a genuine, dedicated researcher originally.

Why this dramatic volte face? What has happened to the human psyche to produce such irrationalities? Is it really just the fear of the unknown and the unexplainable, that twilight zone of uncertainty, that causes this? What happens to the clear thinking, logical mind? Will it ever return? Is there some more sinister reason for this abnormal behaviour? Does the phenomenon (just as the ideas of Copernicus, Galileo and Darwin did in their times) pose such a threat to our ordered society, Church and Government that concerted attempts have to be made to discredit crop circles and all who study them?

LAST REBUTTALS

Before we go on to examine the physical and mental effects real formations can have on those who visit them – ranging from rapid healing of ailments to violent nausea and sickness – here are a final few stories which demonstrate the implausibility of the hoaxers' claims.

A formation appeared in a field of oats on the night of 15 June 1998. The farmer at Privett, Hampshire visited the formation the following day. There had been torrential rain that week and as the farmer walked down the tractor tramline he noticed that it was unmarked. When he looked back over his shoulder, however, his footprints were clearly visible in the waterlogged ground. When he reached the formation he also noticed that there was no mud on the flattened crop, which there would have been if the crop had been flattened by some implement. In his opinion, the only way anyone could have entered the field to make the formation would have been by

Figure 19: Concentric ice formation, Charles River, Massachusetts, January 1991. © *Fortean Times*, no. 74

abseiling. Nevertheless abseilers also would have left tell-tale evidence of mud on the fallen plants.

Abseiling would also have been the only method anyone could have used to create a snow formation which appeared outside Moscow – all around the formation was virgin snow: there was not a single mark or trace of a footprint leading to or from the circle.

Often sceptics ignore these straightforward physical facts in their keenness to dismiss anything of a bizzare or unexplained nature. Circles in ice have been reported from 1930 onwards, in places as diverse as Sweden, Canada and the Ukraine.

Peter Williams (as reported in the *Fortean Times*, no. 74), suggests that they are made by people using 'an ice-saw, an adapted chainsaw used in ice manufacture since its invention in the 1920s'. One person would stand at the centre with a length of rope with which to guide a second person, who would slice an inner and outer ring in the ice with a saw, holding the other end of the rope as taut as possible. The ring would then be broken up, and the ice disk released. However, what Peter fails to take into account is the fact that several of the reports state that the ice was too thin to bear any human weight, let alone that of any extra equipment.

This story illustrates the sheer physical problems

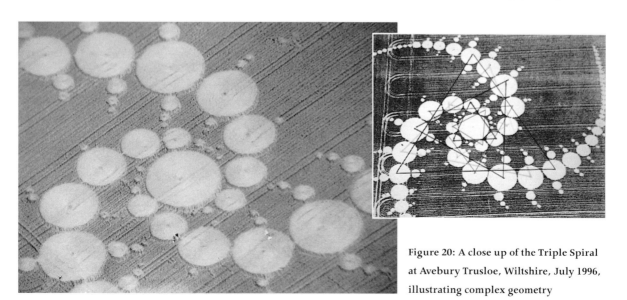

Figure 20: A close up of the Triple Spiral at Avebury Trusloe, Wiltshire, July 1996, illustrating complex geometry

Figure 21: 'Handkerchief'. East Field, Alton Barnes, Wiltshire, 9 July 1998. Diameter *c.*300 ft (91m). Wheat

Figure 22: © Barry Reynolds

hoaxers must explain away when claiming that formations are all man-made. One example from 1996 may suffice. The mighty Triple Spiral at Avebury Trusloe was made up of three arms, totalling 194 perfectly graded circles spiralling out from the centre and extending to a diameter in excess of 1,000 feet (303m). This formation also consisted of a series of equilateral triangles, spiralling, rotating and expanding from the centre outwards in quite awesome precision.

This geometric exactitude alone makes this almost impossible to replicate exactly (bearing in mind that it would have to be laid out in the dark and without disturbing the surrounding crop). There is also the problem of vision limitation in a large field of mature corn – if you have ever stood in a field of ripe corn you will know that you can only see a few feet in front of you at most: the sea of corn prevents any sense of perspective, merging into a mass. The only way to lay out a complex pattern in such a field would be from an aerial view. The time element is also important. Even if we allow 10 minutes to flatten each circle, 194 circles would take over 32 hours!

In a television programme on the subject, one particular hoaxer initially claimed that this formation was easy to replicate. However, when challenged to reproduce the formation exactly, he refused. (Interestingly, when the programme was broadcast, this refusal was inexplicably edited out.)

The above diagram (Figure 22, supplied by Sussex researcher Barry Reynolds, together with the calculations; *Sussex Circular* 81, Nov/Dec 1998) illustrates the implausibility of the hoaxers' claims. The diagram is based on the amount of time it would take two men, using an ordinary 30-inch (0.75m) garden roller, to create the 300-foot (91m) diameter East Field Handkerchief formation at Alton Barnes, Wiltshire, of 1998, walking at 2.5 mph (4 kph).

One rotation of the roller would create a 5-foot (1.5m) circle. For a circle of 300 feet (91m) diameter, covering 1.6 acres (0.7ha), you would have to walk round in circles 60 times following the lay of the crop, covering well over 28,000 feet (8485m) – or 5.3 miles (8.5km)! It would take the two over two hours just to roll the crop flat, without allowing time to sculpt the magnificent scalloped edge. There are also 147 small circles dotted round the edge. Although I would reckon on 10 minutes per circle, Barry is more generous and calculates that each circle would take just three minutes to create, which still adds up to an additional 7 hours and 20 minutes – nearly 9 ½ hours in total!

Bearing in mind that this formation appeared at night, in silence, with perfect geometry and with people watching the field all the time, it does overstretch the limits of logical reasoning if we are being asked to believe it could have been made by man.

Figure 23: The 'Mitsubishi' formation

Who Wants to be Taken for a Ride?

In 1998 two young men were hired, at considerable cost, to make a crop formation resembling a Mitsubishi car for an advertisement. They were seen labouring in the top side of East Field, Alton Barnes. They did not seem to be relishing the task; nor did they seem to know exactly what they were doing – they kept shouting at each other and clearly found the job difficult. They became hot, sweaty and increasingly bad tempered.

Despite having obtained the farmer's permission, and therefore safe in the knowledge that they were in no danger of being caught in an act of criminal damage, they took two whole days to complete the job.

THE FINAL DOUBT DISPELLER

In 1994 two formations appeared in barley at Birling Gap, near Eastbourne, looking like suspended cobwebs. The formations consisted of two rather ordinary looking elements: one oval shaped, the other resembling a teardrop with the bottom sliced off. However, as soon as we got closer, we saw that the barley had been bent uniformly down at around 20 inches

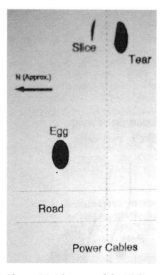

Figure 24: Diagram of the Birling Gap oval formation, 20 June 1994. Barley. © Barry Reynolds

(50cms) up from the ground – about half way down each stalk and just above the point where the leaf separates from the sheath. As the top part of the crop bent over it had formed myriad small vortices, each measuring 12–15 inches (30–38cms) in diameter, tightly interwoven and, in turn, forming part of the overall webbing. The complexity of the webbing was astounding, and its density was such that it was difficult and painful to try and pierce by walking through it.

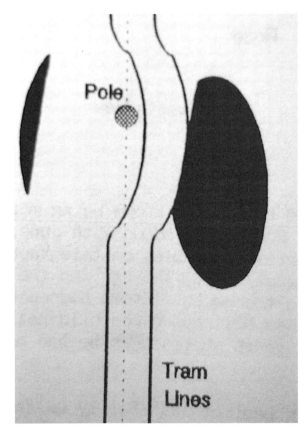

Figure 25: Diagram of the sliced formation.

© Barry Reynolds

The Tear-drop formation (in the same field) was even more puzzling. Constructed in the same manner as the oval, it lay divided beneath a power line, directly under the telegraph pole, straddled on either side of the tramlines. One part of the severed formation measured 27 feet (8.1m); could the rest of the formation on the other side of the tramline be the missing piece? Yes, indeed ... it measured 27 feet 2 inches (8.2m)!

It seemed as though the pole had acted as a screen, deflecting and possibly distorting the electromagnetic field, hitting the power line and slicing the formation in two as it came down. For 'down' it must have come, as had it come from below, the power line would not have caused a problem.

So what could have been responsible? Could a tightly focused sonic beam of high intensity be the culprit?

Clearly the circle could not have been made by any sort of weight (eg a garden roller or a flail), because the crop would have been flattened. An unknown atmospheric condition? This would not explain the many tiny vortices merging to give the overall effect of one great web, enclosed in a circumference with such a clear cut off point between the webbing and the standing crop beyond. Rook or crow damage? An example of this was nearby, and displayed no uniform bending of the barley, no complex webbing, and had many feathers and droppings scattered among the randomly and chaotically damaged barley. Nor do rooks normally carry tape measures! Very localized wind damage? Again there was an example of this nearby, and the crop was splayed sideways randomly – very different to the concise pattern in the formation.

This crop formation seems to defy all logical explanation. Indeed, whatever the 'force' responsible, it seems to 'place' crop circles on the ground from above: formations on hill slopes are elliptical, not circular, with the degree of the ellipse corresponding exactly to the gradient of the slope. The force at Birling Gap appears to have been genetically selective as well! A few rogue stalks of winter wheat from the previous year's crop were not affected. They remained standing, clearly visible above the twisted barley. What force could create such an elaborate and dense suspended barley webbing, and yet leave single stems of wheat untouched?

Man-made formations do exist, but certainly *not* on the scale that the hoaxers wish us to believe.

Figure 26: Birling Gap, showing a single stalk of standing wheat

Chapter Three

Physical and Emotional Effects

The physical effects experienced by people who have entered crop circles are many and varied. They range from the unpleasant, such as headaches, nausea, dizziness and tiredness, through to many cases of healing and increased well-being.

It is hard to know exactly why there should be such varied reports. Dowsers tell us that there is a network of energy lines running through the earth. That we each have our own energy field is now accepted; indeed, all living things emit energy. (Our brains give off complex electrical signals which can be measured on an electro-encephalogram (EEG). The effects of those charges on our physical and emotional well-being can be seen and analysed.) It seems to me that people will react in circles according to the way their own energy interacts with whatever energy is inside the circle and the energy aura immediately outside it.

I believe that what happens in a genuine crop formation is that natural energy is drained away, and a replacement energy of varying strength and order is introduced. The strength of this energy field determines its duration. To date there is no machine capable of recording this 'energy', so we have to rely on our diagnostic skills and intuition.

PHYSICAL EFFECTS

Energy Rippling Through my Shoulders

On 15 July 1990 the manner in which my friend Margaret Randall and I reacted to the dumb-bell formation at Morestead, Hampshire was totally unexpected.

Early in the morning, so as to avoid the hot air turbulence that occurs later on on hot summer days, I drove over to Thruxton airport to meet Margaret and my sister, to take some aerial photographs of recent formations. I was in considerable discomfort, having

Figure 27: Pictogram, East Field, Alton Barnes, Wiltshire, 11 July 1990. Wheat. © Alick Bartholomew

Figure 28: Pictogram, Stanton St Bernard, Wiltshire, 11 July 1990. Wheat. © Terence Meaden

damaged my shoulder playing a ferocious game of tennis the previous evening. The pain had been so great that I had been hardly able to lift my arm the previous night.

Once we were airborne, the pilot revealed a wondrous formation below us at Alton Barnes, 350 feet (106m) in length – the sheer size of it, and the complexity of the numerous circles with their abutting spokes, left me absolutely speechless.

It was the first giant pictogram to appear, along with a second one that had been created on the same night in the fields under the White Horse at Stanton

St Bernard. Needless to say, all my aches and pains were totally forgotten!

However, I soon remembered my damaged shoulder whilst driving home, and so we stopped off at Morestead and went into the dumb-bell. Morestead is one of the villages (along with Owlesbury, Baybridge, Marwell and Hensting) that makes up the civil parish of Morestead, covering 5,434 acres (2,200ha), and is recorded in the Domesday Book. We went into the formation and I proceeded in my usual way, dowsing with my pendulum to record the Yin and Yang energies, noting the strength and direction

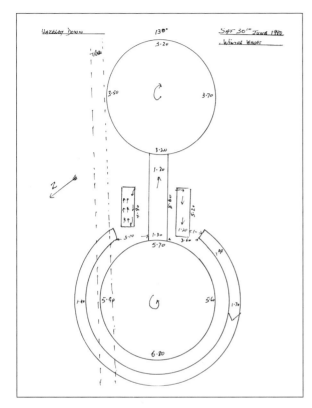

Figure 29: Dumb-bell at Morestead, Hampshire, 30 June 1990. Wheat. © Richard Andrews

Figure 30: Dumb-bell at Morestead, Hampshire, June 1990. © Elizabeth Barnes

of the different energy forces, and also the manner and direction in which the crop lay.

Having almost completed this, I sat down on a strong Yang energy point on the perimeter of the larger circle with great relief. As I was relaxing, I became aware of energy rippling through my shoulders. I gently moved my right shoulder and found to my amazement that I was without pain. I stayed where I was and let the energy continue to flow until my shoulder was completely mobile. I was overjoyed at my recovery.

What happened to Margaret was no less dramatic. When I realized the effect of the circle on me, I called to her and suggested she should come and sit close by. Margaret has the great misfortune to suffer from Raynaud's Phenomenon, a circulatory condition (constrictive, and hence a Yin condition needing the counteraction of Yang energy). I didn't tell her what had happened to me; I simply suggested she might find it a good place to sit. Immediately she expressed a feeling of tremendous well-being and said that her fingers were tingling.

'I can't explain the tingling I experienced in my fingertips except to say it was as if my fingers had been cold, as in a Raynaud's spasm, and that they were warming up – that is, the blood was beginning to flow properly again. But my fingers had not been cold – quite the opposite when one recalls that Sunday was probably one of the hottest days of the summer so far!'

I still had a few things I wanted to check in the configuration, so I left her there. When I returned I found her lying happily on her side with a blissful smile on her face. This she cannot normally do because, as she explains:

'It's rare that Raynaud's Phenomenon is an "illness" by itself; usually there is an underlying cause and in my case it is scleroderma. There are two types of scleroderma: morphoea, which is localized; and systemic sclerosis (which is what I have) and these can affect different organs.

'One of the commonest organs to be affected is the oesophagus; the sphincter muscle to the stomach becomes slack and consequently allows the stomach acids to flow up, thus causing ulcers which, when healed, form strictures thereby narrowing the pipe. This is why I sleep propped up, otherwise it's like having perpetual heartburn! And I didn't get heartburn when lying flat in the crop circle!'

Margaret lay on her side for at least 20 minutes – the first time she was able to lie flat in 15 years – and was most reluctant to leave the circle. After the incident she began to sleep extremely well and her energy noticeably increased. In general she felt a great sense of well-being and there was a continuing marked improvement in her condition. (Margaret is a 'guinea pig' with a London teaching hospital, where her condition is monitored.)

She also, rather hesitantly, remarked how humble the experience of lying in the crop circle had made her feel – as though she had been in the presence of something or someone immense and awesome. I have often had the same, almost inexplicable feeling of wonder and humility. I would like to suggest that when people go into crop circles and are uncertain where to sit, they should let their hearts, not their minds, be their guide.

It was after this remarkable and totally unexpected experience that I decided to channel my energies into researching the physiological and psychological effects of crop circles. Clearly something was happening that warranted further investigation.

Miracles do Happen

Dr Lester Smith was an 88-year-old man with a heart condition and arthritic knee and hip joints. While attending the Glastonbury Conference on Crop

Figure 31: 'The Snail', East Field, Alton Barnes, Wiltshire, 9 July 1992. Wheat. © Jürgen Kronig

Circles during the summer of 1993, he decided that he would visit the Snail Formation in Alton Barnes East Field with a group of others.

There was a dauntingly long walk from the edge of the field into the formation and it often seemed that Dr Smith would not make it. His wife had brought along a chair for him to sit on, which he used periodically. However, he refused to give in, and with considerable difficulty and much help from the others, he eventually reached the formation. Meanwhile a psychic Dutchman in the group had told Mrs Smith that the trouble was in Dr Smith's left hip, and was due to a blockage in his aura.

Sitting on his chair in the formation, Dr Smith silently asked to be put in touch with the 'force' behind the circles. Nothing happened. He decided to be more specific: 'Please take away the pain. Please heal me,' he asked. At that very moment of asking it seemed as though his whole body was suffused with an incredible, ineffable energy, which flooded his whole being. He drank in every drop of the experience, and when the time came for him to leave the formation he walked away with a spring in his step, carrying his chair. (The reality of this experience was confirmed for him the following day when the Dutchman told him that the blockage in the aura had disappeared.)

The humility and simplicity with which Dr Smith recounted his experiences the following day at the Conference was extremely moving.

More Healing

Lesley Clementson has suffered from arthritis since 1969. Over the years more joints have become

arthritic, and both her knees and elbows are painful. Her right hip gives her great discomfort and she is a likely candidate for both hip and knee replacements. She also suffers from diabetes. On 25 May 1992, she entered the formation at Lockeridge in Wiltshire, with her husband Steve and their dog.

'When we entered the field we first went to the single circle, which we felt to be a hoax. In order to reach the other circles we had to follow the

Figure 32a and b (Top): Lockeridge, Wiltshire, 1992, with the standing centre of the largest circle. © Lesley Clementson

tramlines to the top of the field [see Figure 32a].

'As my joints were so painful, I sent Steve on ahead so as not to hold him back. I was walking very slowly and was in so much pain that I was in tears at times. Once inside the circle I just stood still, relieved that I had got there. I remained there for a while, just looking at the beautiful circle.

'After about ten minutes, I began to feel the pain seeping out of my toes. I walked almost pain-free round the circle and into the scroll.

'About an hour later we decided to make our way back down the slope to the road. I wear lace-up shoes in order to be able to loosen them when my feet become uncomfortable. As I walked down the field to the road, I was still almost pain-free and I noticed that my shoes felt as though they were too big. When we reached the road, my shoes needed the laces tightening considerably because the swelling in my feet had gone down almost to normal size.'

Ten days after this experience, the beneficial effects were starting to wear off. However, and despite continuing arthritis, Lesley's feet have not swelled up again even during the hottest days. After almost four months the swelling of her feet and ankles was still reduced by between one-and-a-half to two inches (3–5cms).

There are several reports about the beneficial effects of circles on arthritic and rheumatic pain. Sometimes the pain relief is short-lived, other times it is more lasting. One such sufferer (with two severely arthritic hips and a 'crumbling' knee) was determined to enter the Windmill Hill formation in Hampshire in the summer of 1998, which she eventually managed to do, with considerable difficulty. She and her husband remained in the circle for about 40 minutes, and afterwards she reported that, as she approached the formation she felt as if she had walked 'into a field of well-being', and that coming back she found she was 'walking buoyantly'. Anyone who has any experience of arthritis will know just how astonishing this is.

Another woman, suffering from a condition which, like Parkinson's disease, results in continuous and exhausting shaking, visited the Torus Knot formation that appeared at Alton Priors in July 1997.

She sat in the centre of it for about 20 minutes. She stopped shaking, and did not shake at all for the entire 24 hours afterwards. She reported that the physical relief of not shaking was enormous.

A friend, well into her 80s and suffering from severe and painful osteoporosis, had long begged me to take her into a formation so that she could experience the 'energies' for herself. In June 1997 the Pastry Cutter formation appeared at East Meon, Hampshire near to where she lived.

Early, on a overcast, sultry morning Diana and I walked slowly into the formation. There was an overwelming sense of awe and peace, just as though we had entered a cathedral or other sacred place, which silenced even the normally talkative Diana! By 8 a.m. I had dropped Diana home again, and a couple of hours later she rang me in great excitement – she was totally free of pain! What's more, she is still pain-free over a year on.

It seems that the crop circles and their energy might be acting as some sort of anti-imflammation agent. Rheumatism and arthritis both have a core effect of inflammation, and although much more

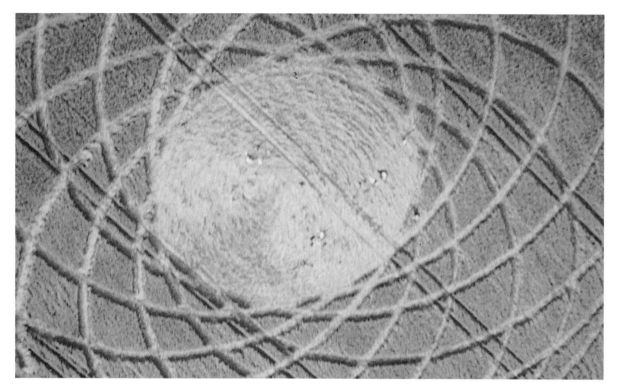

Figure 33: The 'Torus Knot', Alton Priors, Wiltshire. 11 July 1997. Wheat. Close up of the centre. The formation stretches to a diameter of over 500 feet (152m)

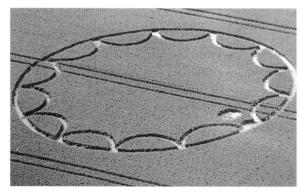

Figure 34: The 'Pastry Cutter', East Meon, Hampshire, 29 June 1997. Wheat

research needs to be done on this aspect of crop formations, it may be that, by reducing the inflammation, the 'energy' reduces the pain and stiffness caused by these particular diseases – just as the mineral copper does.

The East Meon Pastry Cutter was not the only formation to silence visitors, with its 'Cathedral effect' – the 1997 Star of David formation at Silbury had the same impact on a charming and vociferous Italian photographer whom I showed round. It was his first visit to a crop formation, and the only thing he was able to utter was 'Astounding! Astounding! Astounding!'

Figure 35: 'Star of David' fractal and Silbury Hill, 23 July 1997. 390 ft (118m) diameter, 126 circles. Wheat.

On occasions it seems that healing can result from a bad experience in a crop circle, as in the case of a woman with a long-standing pain in her left shoulder. She visited a formation in Wiltshire.

'While I was in the circle, sitting near the centre of the formation, the pain in my left shoulder and wrist became intense. Gradually the whole of my left arm, hand and the left part of my chest became very hot. It was as if I was very conscious of that part of my body. On leaving the formation, and for a couple of hours afterwards, my left arm felt slightly "dead".

'Later in the evening the symptoms totally receded, and from the next morning, and for several days afterwards, the chronic pain I had suffered previously disappeared. The same effects were felt in another circle and in both cases I felt somehow exhausted.'

Interestingly, there are stories of healings arising from visits to formations known to be man-made. Whether the sufferers expect to be healed, and therefore are, or whether the hoaxers either accidentally or deliberately construct their circles on natural energy lines, no one can tell. One such story comes from a Canadian woman suffering from Carpal Tunnel syndrome, where the meridian nerve that runs down the forearm to the wrist becomes trapped. In severe cases it can lead to complete numbness of the hand.

In this particular case, the woman had a severe case of the syndrome, her hand being constantly numb. She went into a particular formation and over a period of 40 minutes the numbness wore off totally, nor has it returned.

An Uplifting Experience

One of the ways that genuine crop formations affect people is through the increased nitric oxide levels measured in these formations. Inexpensive government-approved tests, conducted at an analytical laboratory (and costing only around £50), on plants and soil taken from inside formations and compared to control samples have revealed a 2:1 variation in the nitrate/nitrogen content of samples taken from genuine circles.

Nitric oxide, although associated with acid rain and smog, is a chemical that naturally occurs within our bodies, helping regulate blood pressure and circulation, which perhaps explains the effect that the heightened levels of it experienced in crop circles can have, as one man found out when he visited a circle recently. Much to his amazement (not to mention embarrassment), he had an erection in the formation, which lasted until the next day. Who needs Viagra?!

A Premature Birth

Although many, perhaps the majority of people visiting crop formations experience an increased sense of peace and well-being (if not actual healing), some-

times the effects are not nearly as pleasant. The following report tells of a near tragedy which, thankfully, did have a happy ending. One Sunday afternoon in July 1991, Michael and Karen Neary decided to visit the beautiful Newton St Loe formation, near Bath. It was a glorious day, without a cloud in the sky. Michael takes up the story.

'Karen was approximately 27 weeks pregnant at the time and had had no problems with her pregnancy at all. We parked in the field adjacent to the formation, paid our fee, then eagerly followed the tramlines to the pictogram.

'What you feel on entering is very difficult to describe. For Karen, she knew she was "in" the circle before noticing the physical reality of it — the flattened crop, swirls, circle walls and so on. The baby also seemed to know. It jumped! Very quickly and very suddenly! It was as if the child

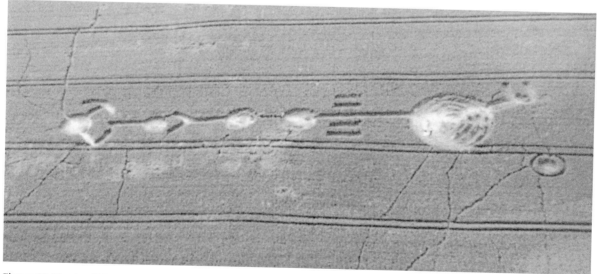

Figure 36: Newton St Loe, Somerset, July 1991. © Jürgen Kronig

had stretched out its arms and legs in an instant, to its full extent. After this the baby became calmer although Karen said it was moving in a strange way, rocking itself perhaps.

'My reaction on entering the formation was a feeling of sudden awareness or clarity of mind, like having an extension to reality in an instant, which lasted for a few seconds before returning to normal. If I never stood in a crop circle again that experience would be enough for me.'

Everything was normal when Karen and Michael went home that evening. However, by the next morning the previous day's events were forgotten as Karen was taken to hospital where doctors fought to stop the birth of a very premature baby. The battle was won and Karen was allowed home the following Friday. She immediately gave up her job and took things easy for the remainder of her pregnancy. The doctors suggested many reasons for what happened. They thought she might have over-exercised, although she thought this unlikely as she had been walking to work (40 minutes a day) with no ill effects.

Rachael was eventually born on 12 October, weighing 5lbs 5ozs (4.8kg). Despite being a first child, it was an easy birth. In fact, Rachael was an astonishingly easy baby, sleeping through the night at just a month old. However, I would have to agree with Karen and Michael, and advise anyone who is pregnant against visiting a crop formation.

Unpleasant Physical Effects

Although 90 per cent of the time I feel extremely well in crop formations (and, in fact, have grown to expect that I will feel well), I have to admit that for the remaining 10 per cent of the time I do not. Others also have had unpleasant reactions to circles, ranging from violent nausea, headaches and migraines, to a general feeling of lethargy and 'unwellness'.

Over a period of 48 hours in 1991, I took a couple of people to the Upham Insectogram formation near Bishops Waltham, Hampshire, and we all had violent negative reactions.

The first person was actress Sarah Miles. At 5 a.m., at the beginning of a beautiful June day, we entered the formation together with a deep sense of reverence at the magical stillness and wonder of being part of the awakening world. We were wet from the moisture in the air and, despite warm clothing, could feel the chill. I made straight for one of the two spots that I had previously dowsed for compatible energies. Sarah found her 'own' place and we lost ourselves in the majesty of the sunrise, the awakening birds and the scuttling of field mice, voles and large insects. The larks were the latest risers, not proclaiming their existence until shortly after 6 a.m. By then the mist had gone and the sun was beaming down on us. It seemed as though the whole world was smiling.

Suddenly Sarah shot up, feeling instantly and acutely nauseous. We immediately left the formation and went back to the car. As soon as we did so, Sarah felt completely well and came home for some breakfast. At the time I put her nausea down to getting up early and having had nothing to eat.

The next day I took Canadian Michelle Veseau to visit the formation. About 20 yards away from the edge of the circle she stopped short, as though she had met a solid 'wall'. Worse was to follow: when we reached the perimeter of the 'body' of the Insec-

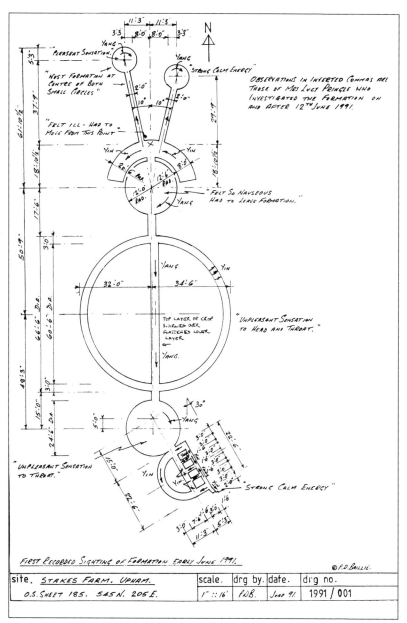

Figure 37: Drawing of the 'Insectogram', Upham, near Bishops Waltham, Hampshire, June 1991. © Peter Baillie

togram, she keeled over and lay prostrate on the ground. I thought something dreadful had happened, but she reassured me and said she just needed to lie quietly for five minutes. I went to one of my 'safe' spots and waited. Ten minutes later Michelle was still lying there, oblivious to everything. Eventually she stirred and got up. As she did so, such violent nausea overtook me that I called to Michelle, made a dash out of the formation and ran away as fast as I could. The immediate and violent nature of the nausea took me completely by surprise, until I remembered Sarah's identical reaction the previous morning.

The Julia Set opposite Stonehedge (which had appeared so quickly in the summer of 1996, *see Chapter 1, page 12*), had very bad effects on many people. On 9 July I took two friends to visit it. They entered quite happily, but for some reason I was unwilling to enter and turned back to the car. Shortly afterwards, although they recovered within a few minutes, my friends both returned, pea-green with nausea. That weekend friends from Canada reported that they had experienced varying degrees of physical and psychological discomfort when in the formation on the Friday, including nausea, severe fatigue, and an inability to think or remember things. A young Irishman, on his first visit to a crop formation reported on the effects:

> 'Felt very similar to feeling of intense ultraviolet radiation or gamma radiation, both of which I am familiar with as a molecular biologist working in that field. Experienced initial nausea [which lasted] all day until I went to sleep. Several hours later experienced intense physical well-being and mental clarity.'

Negative rather than beneficial effects are more easily recognized, so it is very interesting that he remarked on his increased physical and mental well-being; clearly it was of such a marked degree it could not be ignored.

Over the weekend thousands of other people visited the formation, and when my Canadian friends and I returned to it on the Monday, none of us suffered any unpleasant effects. Could it be that the many visitors had acted as 'blotting paper', soaking up all the formation's energy over the weekend? American researcher Nancy Talbot also had a bad reaction to the Lozenge pictogram at East Kennett in 1993. She had felt uneasy about going into the formation and 'defacing its powerful beauty', but had entered it after all, against her better judgement. She did not feel unwell whilst inside the formation, and it was not until the next morning that she realized something was wrong. She was 'literally unable to get out of bed, had difficulty breathing, and found myself lying on my bed concentrating hard on simply

Figure 38: Lozenge, East Kennett, near Marlborough, Wiltshire, 24 July 1993. Wheat.

getting the job of breathing done.' Thankfully, she had recovered by the following day.

Nancy's account reinforces my belief that people will react very differently to the energies present within formations, and they should not linger inside a formation if they feel at all unwell.

PSYCHOLOGICAL EFFECTS

The reports in this book have been submitted by ordinary, normal, sane and sensible people. They have experienced effects that have taken them totally by surprise and quite contrary to their expectations.

Patricia Rhodes from the Isle of Wight is, by all accounts, a remarkably good natured and happy person. In 1990 five circles appeared near Hasely Manor on the Isle of Wight; two in one field and a triangular threesome in an adjacent field. In July she visited the largest single circle.

'As I approached the circle, I found myself involuntarily smiling and feeling very happy. I stood in the centre and felt very comfortable, and found I was grinning and couldn't stop!'

However, a week later, Patricia had a very different experience in the same formation.

'I stepped into No. 2 circle of the threesome and felt immediate anger. It was messy, whereas the other two circles were smooth and beautiful. I rationalized that this was why I felt angry, although I knew that was stupid. I quickly stepped outside the circle feeling confused and churned up.

'I went to step into the circle a second time; I felt very apprehensive, but did so anyway and once again felt angry. I stepped out and went into the two other circles where I had no reaction.'

A friend who had been in the circles in the other field, also entered the No. 2 circle and immediately called out to Patricia that she, too, felt 'angry'. There had been no prior conversation between the two about how Patricia had felt.

In June 1991, a beautiful rape seed circle appeared in the same place as the threesome of the previous year. Again Patricia and a friend went to have a look.

'I only learnt about it through the local paper, so by the time I arrived with my friend, the crop had begun to send up new shoots and it all looked rather tired.

'The moment I entered the circle, I wanted to get out. It felt oppressive, smothering and I found myself wringing my hands constantly. I had never been in a rape crop before and I might have been reacting to it. Compared to the previous year, though, the effect was only mildly unpleasant.'

Her friend also felt uncomfortable, although not to the same extent.

What energy was Patricia experiencing? A residual energy from the previous year, or a new kind? Many people ask how long the 'energy' remains after a crop circle has formed? We don't know the answer; however, I took a friend of mine into a secondary growth formation in February one year. He developed such a violent headache he had to come out. He is not a man who is prone to headaches.

Covert Activity?

There seems to be a general feeling, which can reach paranoid proportions, that the circles are the subject of government covert activity.

In July 1990 a Russian woman, Lydia, from Krasnoyarsk in Siberia, together with a friend, came upon an oval, spirally flattened in the grass in a meadow in the middle of a birch wood. They had never seen anything like it, so examined it more closely and reported that 'the air above the oval seemed to be a few degrees colder that the surroundings'. Both she and her friend also experienced unsettling and disturbing sensations whilst in the oval, which lasted over an hour.

A physics teacher, to whom Lydia reported the phenomenon, remarked that crop circles like the one she described were fairly common and appeared around Krasnoyarsk every year. Although the teacher was certain that the circles were a natural phenomenon, others were not so sure. The general feeling was that the circles were of a paranormal nature, and that the then Soviet government 'was carrying out secret research into the subject using parapsychologists as well as conventional scientists'. They were also convinced that the government were keeping the whole thing secret. It is interesting to note that Krasnoyarsk and the surrounding area was completely 'closed' to foreigners until 1991.

Figure 39: The Beckhampton Triangle, Wiltshire, July 1990. Wheat. © Pat Delgado

We were Enchanted

A whole book could be devoted to understanding the psychology of the crop circle phenomenon and its emotional undercurrents. That our emotions play a powerful part in determining our actions, either consciously or unconsciously, is demonstrated daily, sometimes with the most unexpected results.

Ralph Noyes, who was until 1972 the Under-Secretary of State in the Defence department, heading Defence Secretariat 8 (DS8) whose work included handling UFO reports from the public (and who sadly died in 1998), described how he was inexplicably affected while in the Triangle at Beckhampton in early August 1990. He had visited this formation with some friends on Sunday 5 August after most of the weekend crowds had gone.

Ralph was blessed with an amazingly clear and brilliant mind, which pierced any situation like a laser beam, separating fact from fiction, truth from falsehood. What happened to him that August evening left him in such a turmoil that for almost two years he refused to write about his experience, hoping for a rational explanation. At the end of this time, realizing that no such clarification was going to be forthcoming, he bravely put pen to paper.

'We spent a little time in the Scrolls nearby and then entered the Triangle. A feeling of something highly energetic was greatly reinforced in the Triangle. I also had a strong visual impression of a river of energy flowing through the Triangle from about north, north-east to south, south-west. It looked like a ceaseless flow of bright particles, each one of which persisted only long enough to cover a foot or two [30–60cms] but was immediately succeeded by another. The analogy that occurred to me was of the flow of atomic and sub-atomic particles through the old-fashioned Bubble Chamber in which physicists used to make tiny specks briefly visible. I asked Alick and Mari if they saw the same thing. They didn't. I concluded that I wasn't seeing anything "out there", but that my visual cortex (or some other part of my "inner" perceptual apparatus) was being affected by an otherwise invisible source of energy.

'All three of us, I think, found ourselves addictively gripped by the Triangle. We must have remained in it for up to an hour and a half, standing to start with, but eventually kneeling and then lying down. I am reporting, not interpreting: it must be for others to consider whether we had suggested ourselves into a state of "wonder"; there was, after all, a great full moon rising and we were looking at events which were, at the least, surprising. What I must report is that for me (and I think my companions) the occasion felt momentous. We were enchanted or englamoured in a manner that seems to resemble the experiences reported from folklore in which mortal man makes the mistake of engaging with the faery folk! I wouldn't have been too sorry to remain there forever, neglecting all the mundane obligations and accidents with which we have to cope.

'I must also report that the experience was, on the whole, disturbing. I didn't like the "addictive" feel, and the experience seemed to me to be as potentially disruptive of our wholesome concern for the daily management of ourselves and our planet as, say, drug-dependence or too much attachment to one's hypnagogic imagery or dream life.'

Ralph did suffer occasionally from mild migraines which, he said, seem to be related as much to the weather as to anything else that he might be doing. They were not severe enough to be disabling.

HUMAN INTERACTION WITH FORMATIONS

One of the most bizarre aspects of the crop circle phenomenon is human interaction with the circles. Indeed, many people feel curious effects even in formations that we strongly suspect to be man-made.

It might not be too strange if all the effects were beneficial, for it seems rational to suppose that most people look forward to a trip to see a crop circle. Normally, this is a time when they will be away from the hassles of daily life, the weather is likely to be good, the scenery delightful and they can relax happily. But this is NOT the case.

That more reports of adverse effects are received than of beneficial ones is not in itself conclusive. I have been into over 300 formations and have felt ill in possibly 10 per cent of them. Whereas I have written reports relating to those occasions, I have not written reports on the many other times I felt perfectly well for, as Cleve Backster found out: 'stimuli are more readily observable when they evoke emotions related to the negative effect on the well-being of the donor. Emotions related to positive effects on the well-being of the donor generally do not seem to be as easily observable.' ('Biocommunication Capability at a Distance between Human Donors and Invitro Oral Leukocytes', 1985) Some of the following stories will give an indication of what may be happening. In every case, the effect seems to have been unexpected and unpredictable.

In the spring of 1995 I went into a formation that I had good reason to distrust as a hoax, yet as I was walking down one of the paths I was overwhelmed by a feeling of nausea. I tried to persuade myself that this was stupid and could not be happening, but to no avail and I had to make a rapid exit. I recovered almost immediately, but I was not prepared to repeat the experiment. Admittedly I was walking against the lay of the crop at the time, which has been the case in the majority of occasions when I have felt unwell in a formation. (I have subsequently had several other similar, independent reports of people feeling unwell when walking against the flow of the flattened crop.)

Jürgen Kronig, political correspondent for *Die Zeit* in Germany, sent me another story which is of interest for several reasons. In 1993 a group of twenty film students from Frankfurt came over to England to visit and investigate crop and stone circles for their studies.

On 11 July a crop circle appeared overnight at Waden Hill along Avebury Avenue. The next morning the students visited the formation. Eighteen of the twenty experienced unusual effects, either negative or positive; some developed headaches, some felt dizzy, whereas others experienced beneficial effects.

Kronig had asked them about their attitude towards crop circles before they arrived in England. Half had declared their belief that all crop formations were man-made, whereas the other half were open to non-normal explanations, yet despite these divided opinions 90 per cent of the students experienced some effect or other.

A further point of interest is that, unknown to the students, there was good reason for suspecting that this particular formation had been man-made.

Collective Interactions

Chad Deetken, a Canadian researcher, went into the Watmough formation in the Province of Saskatchewan. It had appeared on a farm in August 1990.

Chad and two companions entered the Watmough configuration, and each laid down in a different section of the complex. It was a brisk but pleasant night, and star-gazing and searching for the Aurora Borealis were a convenient excuse for their visit, although the actual purpose was to see what, if anything, might be seen, heard or experienced that was out of the ordinary.

All three people lying in the formation experienced something unusual at exactly the same time – although this was not established until after the event. After spending some time in the formation, Chad began to experience a tension in his muscles, which increased until his breathing became difficult. This tension was so acute that he was forced to sit up and, on so doing, he became quite dizzy. As he was sitting up, he noticed that one of his companions, quite a distance away, was shining a flashlight around the area, as if looking for something.

Later, Chad questioned the two separately about what, if anything, they had experienced while in the formation. Both told him, independently, that whenever they closed their eyes, they clearly and distinctly heard the sound of footsteps. It was the sound of someone walking on the dry, flattened wheat stalks in the pathways, and it seemed to be very close. When asked why one of them had been shining the flashlight around, he replied that he was afraid someone or something was going to step on him.

Nobody Else was There

The final story comes independently from two sources. A woman was sitting in a crop circle with a group of others, quietly meditating on the perimeter of a formation. She had recently damaged her back and was unable to bend. The journey there had seemed long and painful, and it had been difficult for her to walk up the field from where her car was parked.

Having heard of other healing successes in crop circles, she hoped she might also be lucky. She closed her eyes and tried to relax. As she was meditating, she heard footsteps coming up behind her and someone sitting down.

When the meditation finished she remained seated on the ground and looked around for the person who had joined her. There was no one in addition to the group she was with. The man sitting next to her turned to her and asked: 'Where is the person who sat down behind us?' He had also heard footsteps and someone sitting down. But nobody else was there!

The happy ending to this strange tale is that the woman was healed. She can now bend easily – 'even to the point of touching my toes!'

POSSIBLE PHYSIOLOGICAL EXPLANATIONS

What curious interaction is occurring? What influence is creating these contradictory and independently reported effects? As these emotional effects form such an important aspect of crop circle phenomena, an explanation of the physiological aspect of what might be happening is perhaps in order.

It is accepted that different levels of consciousness exist and all are vital to our make up. These can be seen on an encephalogram, a recording of the basic rhythms or electrical signals generated by the brain. These comprise the Beta, Alpha, Theta and Delta rhythms.

The Beta rhythm, at 13–30 Hz, is the normal waking pattern of the brain and is associated with active thinking and problem-solving of a concrete nature. It is the outside window to the world.

The Alpha rhythm, 8–13 Hz, is the most difficult to analyse. The late Maxwell-Cade (in *The Awakening Mind*), describes it as the 'no mind' state, indicating only a peripheral awareness of things which are going on around, but which is easily 'snapped' out of if unfamiliar noises, worries or thoughts intrude. Einstein was able to solve complex mathematical problems while in an Alpha state.

The Alpha state develops during adolescence, not becoming fully stabilized until around the age of 18. It can be accessed though relaxation and meditation, and used to control pain – there have been many wonderful examples of this in which the need for pain-relieving drugs has been eliminated.

In normal consciousness the brain seems to be kept synchronized by short bursts of Alpha waves, interspersed with Beta waves of activity. This is the case for 70 per cent of people – the 'Responsive' types.

The Theta rhythm, 4–7 Hz, appears in meditative and dream-like states. It is also present when dowsers are working. It is associated with accessing unconscious material through hypnosis, creative insight and deep meditation. It is also in the Theta state that one experiences those magical and elusive moments in the intermediate state between sleeping and waking, when one is aware of being in an altered dimension or reality, in which one's own everyday self is being transported to a higher state, seeing, sensing and understanding beyond our normal comprehension. The Delta rhythm, 1/2–4 Hz, is usually represented by deep sleep.

The electromagnetic wave of frequency encircling the planet at the level of the stratosphere, and known as the Schumann Resonance is 7.38 Hz. The Schumann Resonance also corresponds to the Theta wavelength frequency of the human brain, and that would suggest that some strange effects would be produced when someone's brain frequency centres on it. Heightened activity would be expected in everyone and some people will have intense feelings of 'at-oneness' with everybody and the whole of nature. Others would be provoked into a blind, berserker fury or mad dancing frenzies. The reaction will largely depend on the nature of the person, whether they are an extrovert or an introvert.

Lunar and Tidal Effects

The lunar cycle of 29 ½ days from new moon to new moon has a profound effect on many living species, principally because of the tidal phenomena associ-

Figure 40: Angus Pringle demonstrating how a pendulum is pulled off the vertical in the centre of Ogbourne Maizey pictogram, Wiltshire, July 1991.

ated with the lunar phases. The tide-raising power of the Sun is about one-third that of the Moon, each body trying to produce two high tides in the Earth's oceans, one directly below it and the other on the opposite side of the Earth. Thus, when we have a new or full moon, all three bodies are in line, so that the Moon and Sun are collaborating with their tide-raising powers, producing the very high and very low tides known as the spring tides. At the first- and third-quarter Moon phases, however, Sun and Moon are in tidal 'enmity'. The Moon is stronger but its tide-raising powers are noticeably reduced, giving neap tides.

Turtles and other marine organisms in their life cycles are strongly influenced by such lunar and solar gravitational interplays on the oceans of the Earth. There are of course similar tides in the Earth's atmosphere, and small but measureable ones in the solid material of the Earth itself. There may well be additional effects we have not yet discovered.

The gravitational effects of genuine crop circles can be shown by use of pendulums. In one formation at Ogbourne Maizey in Wiltshire, a pendulum was dragged 15–20 degrees off vertical in the centre of the circle by a deviation in the gravitational force.

There is an internationally accepted value by which it can be calculated how long it will take a suitably weighted pendulum attached to a certain length of chain, the top of which is secured to a fixed point, to make one complete swing. Ted Richards, an ex-naval Ministry of Defence scientist, suggests that if that value were to vary either way, plus or minus, the pendulum would either accelerate or decelerate accordingly.

What do we Really Know about Gravity?

Keith Wakelam suggests that 'We know that gravity is a force. It is the mutual attraction (action) between two masses, varying as the inverse square of distance between them $m1 \times m2/d2$. For example the Moon, being of smaller mass than the mass of the Earth, is drawn towards the Earth, but is kept in an elliptical orbit around the Earth by its own angular momentum, which balances the gravitational attraction, rather [like] a ball on a piece of string. But for these characteristics, it would crash headlong into the Earth or fly off into space. But although small, the Moon causes the Earth to revolve around a Barycentre on a common centre of mass.'

If the genuine circles are producing strong magnetic and gravitational anomalies within them, above them and in their vicinities, we should not be surprised to find bewildering and disturbing phenomena appearing to us when we visit circles. There could well be noticeable effects on the electro-chemical processes within our bodies.

Effects of Hormonal Changes

The pituitary and pineal glands (both connected to the hypothalamus region of the brain), secrete hormones such as melatonin (which is responsible for sleep and sexual cycles), thyroxine (which regulates thyroid (and so energy) levels), oestrogen, progesterone, testosterone, insulin and adrenaline. Changes in levels of these different hormones will produce some of the physical effects that have been reported.

I have been involved in scientific research investigating changes in hormone levels (as well as vitamin and mineral levels) associated with the crop circles. In one such experiment a 72-year old woman and a 54-year old man had their hormone levels measured by Ann Smithells of Biotech Health, Petersfield, Hampshire, using the Best System (BioEnergetic Stress Testing System) before they entered the Windmill Hill formation in Hampshire. They were tested at 12 noon, went into the formation at 2.30 p.m., and were retested at 4.30 p.m. Both of them had significantly increased melatonin levels (indicating pineal gland stimulation), and the man's thyroid level had also greatly increased – indicating pituitary gland stimulation).

The physical effects of exhaustion, increased energy levels, abnormal and post-menopausal bleeding, male erection, racing hearts, panic attacks, extreme hunger, etc, which have all been associated over the years with crop circles, can all be caused by changes in hormone levels

Chapter Four

Remote Effects and Synchronicity

What are 'remote' effects? They are anything and everything that happen away from, but are associated with, the 'scene of the crime'. Some of the effects reported in this chapter started at the time a crop formation was visited, but in other cases the effects were only experienced afterwards – in some cases, quite some time afterwards.

This area of investigation is a veritable and bottomless treasure trove, a cornucopia of mysteries, ranging from the strange clicking, trilling and humming noises associated with the circles, to unexplained time lapses, freak weather conditions, suspension of thought, inability to count, extrasensory perception (ESP), synchronicity and curious dreams – to name but a few. Some of these will be described in this chapter and the next. Some of the happenings are so weird that I felt my spine tingling as the stories were related to me.

Ever since I was a child there have been things and

facts I have known in advance, yet on every occasion these 'knowings' seemed completely normal and fitted in to the general picture of that moment. What we seldom recognize is a shift in realities. For instance, the dream reality is natural at the time it is happening, and when we wake up that reality often lingers until daytime reality takes over. Both realities are legitimate at the time of happening, and so it is with precognition or advance viewing – one has simply moved from one time dimension into another, and unless we make a particular note, we are unaware that anything unusual has occurred.

REMOTE EFFECTS OF CIRCLES

Many people are curious to know whether eating the seeds from inside a crop formation could have any unusual effects. If there were any effects, clearly the amount consumed might make a difference, as would the time at which the seeds were collected, for crop fields are sprayed five times a year, twice with herbicides (September to January and March to May), twice with insecticides (October to December and June to July) and once with fungicides (March to June).

If a field had just been sprayed it would be reasonable to assume that there would be more solution present on the samples than at other times. However, I do not believe that the amount of spray applied (whatever time it was applied) would cause undue effects – after all, the grain is going to be used for human consumption in some form or other.

Barbara Berge, who has experienced the effects of eating grain from circles, grew up in England but has been living in the United States for some time. In 1993 she attended the Glastonbury Crop Circle Conference. She had visited several crop formations previously and in each one had felt 'compelled to eat grain'.

'The first effects of eating the wheat were like having ingested "speed" – that is, high energy, sleeplessness, nervousness and loss of appetite. I experienced this after about the second day of eating it. By the fifth day (the last day of the conference) I was "flying" – and it happened very suddenly. I remember walking along a street in Glastonbury when I was overcome by a feeling of total cellular vibration. I stopped and stared at my hands because of what felt like streams of energy pouring out of my palms. It was like the tingling sensation one gets after a limb has "gone to sleep" and the blood starts to flow into it again. I found I could not focus on anything and was extremely disoriented.'

Later that day Barbara went to stay with her sister nearby, where the sensations increased to such a degree she became very scared. Sitting on the lawn she 'held on for dear life; letting the energy pour out of me seemed to help'. At the time Barbara did not attribute these sensations to eating the grain. (In fact, Barbara is allergic to wheat; the reaction always takes the form of high mucus production and asthma, but she was taking prescription allergy pills throughout the whole time and not once did she have an asthma attack. However, her allergy does beg the question why she ate the wheat in the first place, which she explains by the strange compulsion she felt – something that others have reported too.)

By the time Barbara flew back to the States that Monday after the Conference, she was feeling the

Figure 41: Seed samples

Cheesefoot Head Punchbowl, Hampshire. 11 July 1987. Wheat. © Terence Meaden

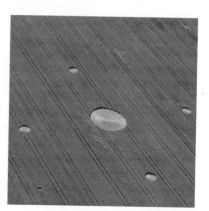

Triple at Beckhampton, Wiltshire.
3 August 1988. Wheat. © Terence Meaden

Quintuplet at Warminster, Wiltshire. 1989. Wheat. © Terence Meaden

Beckhampton, Wiltshire. 7 July 1988.
Wheat. © Terence Meaden

Triple ringer. Warminster, Wiltshire.
Mid-July 1990. Wheat. © John Haddington

'Dumb-Bell'. Doons Law, Perthshire. Mid-August 1990. Wheat. © John Haddington

Silbury, Wiltshire. 1988. Wheat. © Terence Meaden

Silbury with additional circles, Wiltshire. July 1988. Wheat.
© Terence Meaden

Pictogram. East Field,
Alton Barnes, Wiltshire.
11 July 1990. 550 ft
(167 m) long. Wheat.
© Terence Meaden

Pictogram. Stanton St
Bernard, Wiltshire.
11 July 1990. 500 ft
(152 m) long. Wheat.
© Terence Meaden

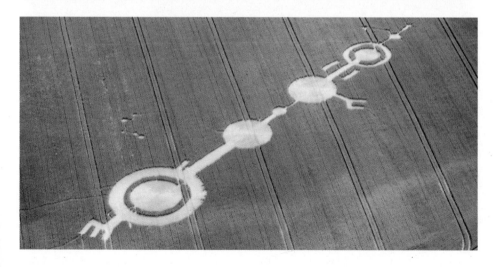

Pictogram. East Kennett,
Wiltshire. 26 July 1990. 300 ft
(91 m) long. Wheat.
© Terence Meaden

Barbury Castle formation and Iron Age hillfort. Wiltshire. 17 July 1991. Wheat. © Jürgen Kronig

'Dancing Man'. Small circle.

'Dancing Man'. Right foot, harvested.

'Dancing Man'. Micheldever, Hampshire. 3 August 1991. 224 ft (68 m) long. Wheat. © Jürgen Kronig

Insectograms. Chilcomb Down, Hampshire. *c.*150 ft (45 m) long. Wheat.
© Andrew King

'The Whale'. Lockeridge, Wiltshire.
30 July 1991. 360 ft (109 m) long. Wheat.

'Vesica Pisces'. The Firs, nr Beckhampton, Wiltshire. 3 August 1991.
128 ft (39 m) long. Wheat.

'The Whale'. Beckhampton, Wiltshire. 1 August
1991. *c.*330 ft (100 m) long. Wheat. © Andrew King

Concentric circles. Woodford, Kettering, Northamptonshire.
7 August 1991. Approx. 250 ft (76 m) diameter. Wheat.
© Stuart and Julie Baker

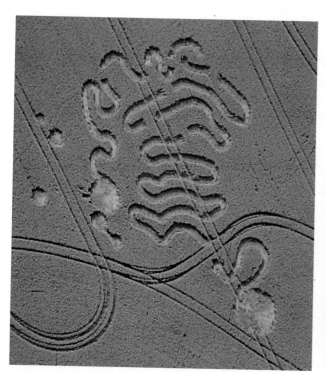

'The Brain'. Froxfield, Wiltshire. 18 August 1991. Wheat.
© Andrew King

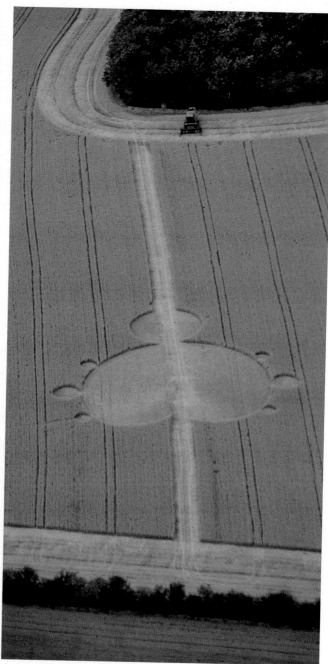

'Mandelbrot Set'. Ickleton, Cambridgeshire. 12 August 1991. 228 ft
(69 m) long, 158 ft (48 m) at widest part. Wheat. © John Haddington

'First Daisy'. Cheesefoot Head,
nr Winchester, Hampshire.
4 August 1991. 56 ft (17 m)
diameter. Wheat. © Jürgen Kronig

'Beetlegram' and 'Second Daisy'. Cheesefoot Head, nr Winchester, Hampshire.
15 and 16 August 1991. Beetlegram 95 ft (29 m) long. Wheat. © Jürgen Kronig

Single ringer. Chilbolton, Hampshire. 12 May 1992.
60 ft (18 m) diameter. Barley.

Single ringer. Broughton, Hampshire. 20 June 1992.
80 ft (24 m) diameter. Wheat.

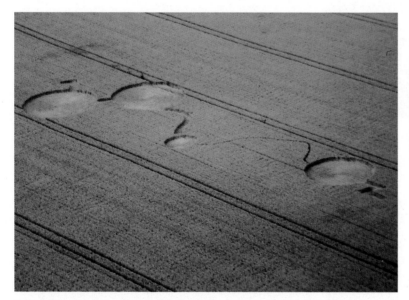

Milk Hill 'Meander' and Paul Vigay. 16 July
1992.

Milk Hill 'Meander'. Alton Barnes, Wiltshire. 16 July 1992. 200 ft (61 m) long.
Circle diameters: L/R 38 ft, 38 ft, 16 ft, 28 ft and 15 ft (12 m, 12 m, 5 m, 8 m
and 5 m respectively). Wheat. © Jürgen Kronig

'Charm Bracelet'. Silbury Hill, Wiltshire.
17 August 1992. 250 ft (76 m) diameter. Wheat.
Above © Andrew King. Other pictures © Grant Wakefield

Early morning in the 'Lunar Crescent' looking towards village. East Dean, nr Chichester, Sussex.

'Solar/Lunar Crescent'. East Dean, nr Chichester, Sussex. 23 July 1994. c.270 ft x 360 ft (82 m x 109 m). Wheat.

Half-miler. Uffington, Oxfordshire.
26 July 1994. *c*.2,500 ft
(756 m) long. Wheat.

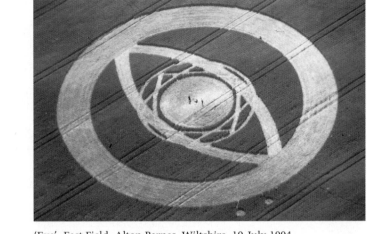

'Eye'. East Field, Alton Barnes, Wiltshire. 19 July 1994.
350 ft (106 m) diameter. Wheat.

'Thought Bubble'. Ipsden, Oxfordshire. 10 July 1994. 144 ft (44 m) long. Wheat. © *Reading Evening Post*

'Spider's Web'. Avebury,
Wiltshire. 10-11 August 1994.
300 ft (91 m) diameter. Wheat.

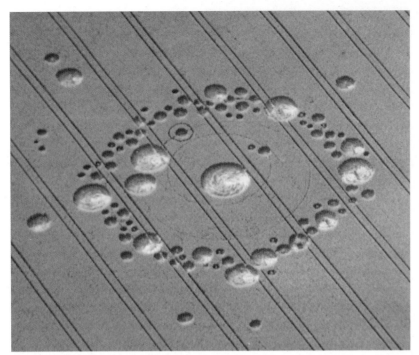

'Asteroid Belt No. 1'. Bishops Sutton, Hampshire. 20 June 1995. *c.*300 ft (91 m) diameter. Four rings, 96 circles. Wheat.

'Asteroid Belt No. 3 The Missing Planet'. Longwood Warren, Hampshire. 26 June 1995. *c.*284 ft (86 m). Six rings, 65 circles in outer ring. Wheat.

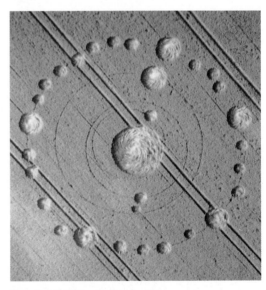

'Asteroid Belt No. 2'. Gander Down, Alresford, Hampshire. 20 June 1995. *c.*200 ft (61 m). Four rings, 32 circles. Wheat.

Pictogram. Overton, Hampshire. 11 May 1995. *c.*200 ft (61 m) long. Oilseed rape.

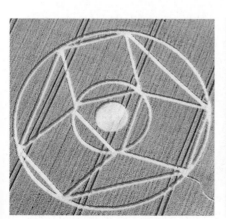

'Cat's Cradle'. Winterbourne Bassett, Wiltshire. 23 July 1995. 140 ft (42 m) diameter. Wheat.

Zig-zag. Cowdown, nr Andover, Hampshire. 18 June 1995. 255 ft (77 m) diameter. Wheat.

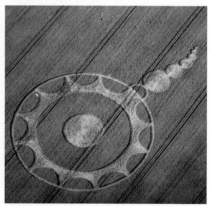

'Venus' Fan'. Danebury hillfort, Hampshire. 16 June 1995. *c.*300 ft (91 m) long. Barley.

'Nautical Wheel'. Crewkerne, Somerset. Late July 1995.
81 ft (25 m) diameter. Wheat.

'Weathervane'. Dorchester, Dorset. Late July 1995.
c.200 ft (61 m) long. Wheat.

'Nested Crescents'. East Meon, Hampshire. Mid-July 1995. 170 ft (52 m) diameter. Wheat.

A   Centre of section of 'Charm Bracelet'. Silbury Hill, Wiltshire. 17 August 1992. Wheat.

B   Centre of small circle. Cheesefoot Head, Hampshire. 12 June 1995. Barley.

C   Centre of satellite circle. Torberry Farm, Sussex. Mid-July 1994. Wheat.

D   Centre of satellite circle, East Meon pictogram. Hampshire. 21 July 1993. Wheat.

E   Centre of circle. East Ilsley, Berkshire. 26 May 1993. Oilseed rape.

F   Centre of small circle, Froxfield pictogram. 9 August 1992. Wheat.

G   Centre of West Kennett circle. 17 June 1992. Wheat.

'Julia Set'. Stonehenge, Wiltshire. 7 July 1996. 919 ft x 508 ft (278 m x 154 m) with 151 circles. Wheat.

'Pisces'. Wayland's Smithy, Ashbury, Oxfordshire. 26 July 1996. 204 ft (62 m) diameter. Wheat.

'Solar/Lunar Eternity Symbol' and 'Caterpillar Fractal'. Liddington Castle, near Swindon, Wiltshire. Caterpillar, c.163 ft x 85 ft (49 m x 26 m) overall. Eternity Symbol, c.140 ft x 163 ft (42 m x 49 m). 29 July 1996.

'Croissant'. Wayland's Smithy, Ashbury, Oxfordshire. 10 August 1996. *c.*228 ft (69 m) long. Wheat.

'The Flower'. Littlebury Green, Essex. 14 July 1996. *c.*280 ft (85 m) diameter. Wheat. © Russell Stannard

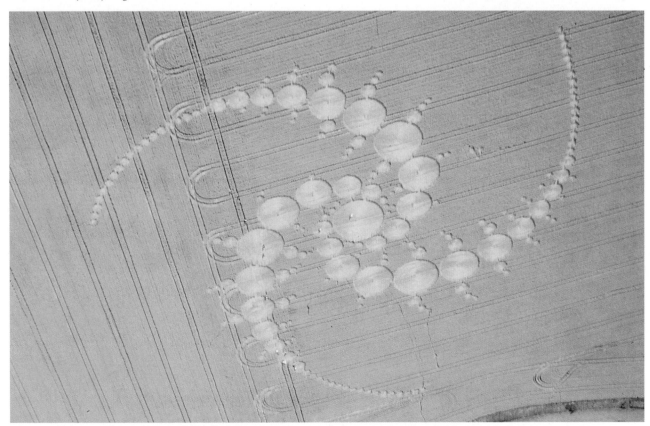

Triple spiral. Windmill Hill, Avebury Trusloe, Wiltshire. 29 July 1996. Over 1,000 ft (300 m) diameter; 194 circles.

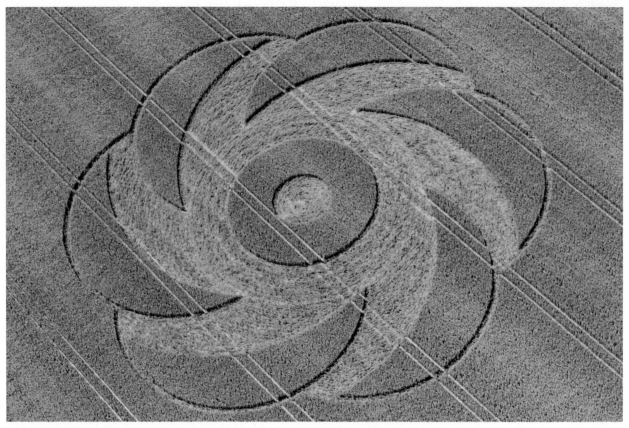

'Flower of Life'. Barbury Castle, Wiltshire. 21 April 1997. 160 ft (48 m) diameter. Oilseed rape.

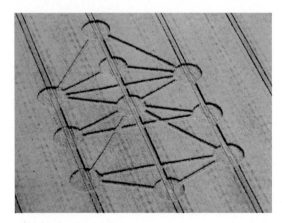

'The Kabbalah'. Barbury Castle, Wiltshire. 1 May 1997. 297 ft (90 m) long, 184 ft (56 m) at widest part. Oilseed rape.

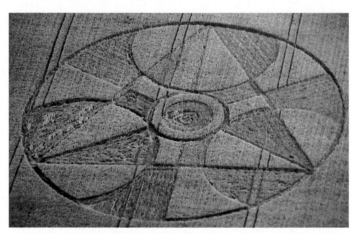

'Florentine Tapestry'. Winterbourne Bassett, Wiltshire. 1 June 1997. 202 ft (61 m) diameter. Barley.

Top left 'Pendant Necklace'. Liddington Castle, nr Swindon, Wiltshire. 3 August 1997. Largest circle 45 ft (14 m) diameter; 29 circles. Wheat.

Middle left 'Gaia'. Upham, Wiltshire. 15 June 1997. *c.*150 ft (45 m) long. Wheat.

Bottom left 'Spinning Star'. Etchilhampton, Wiltshire. 3 August 1997. *c.*180 ft (55 m) diameter. Wheat.

Bottom right 'Mickey Mouse'. Vernham Dean, Hampshire. 2 August 1997. 130 ft (39 m) long. Wheat.

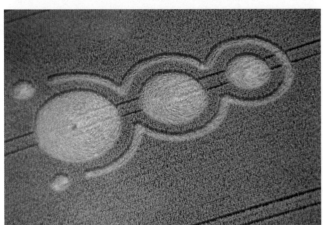

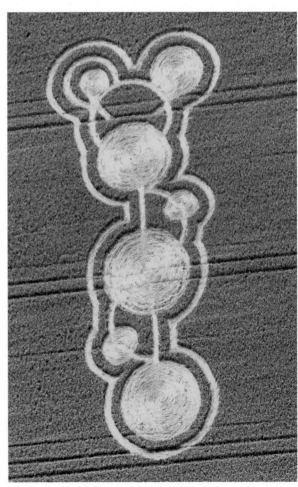

'Earphones'. Liddington Castle, nr Swindon, Wiltshire. Late July 1997. Farmer harvesting. Wheat.

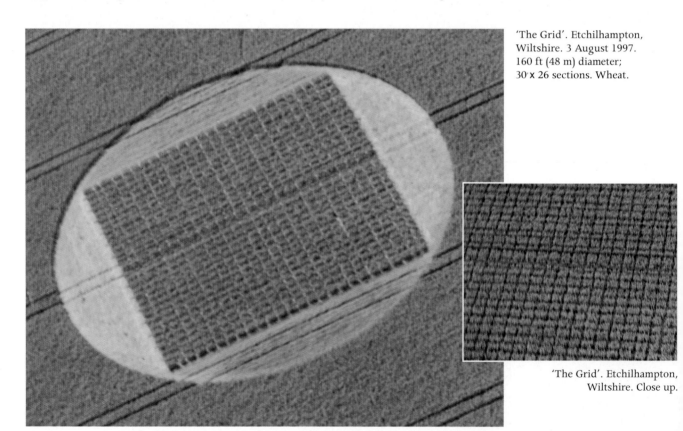

'The Grid'. Etchilhampton,
Wiltshire. 3 August 1997.
160 ft (48 m) diameter;
30 x 26 sections. Wheat.

'The Grid'. Etchilhampton,
Wiltshire. Close up.

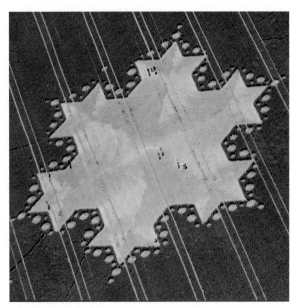

'Star of David' Fractal. Silbury Hill, Wiltshire. 23 July 1997. 390 ft (118 m) diameter; 126 circles. Wheat.

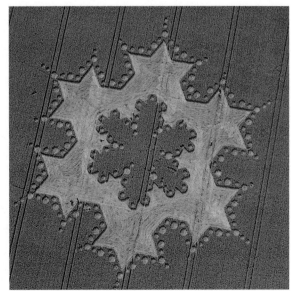

Milk Hill White Horse and Double Fractal. Alton Barnes, Wiltshire.

Double Fractal. Milk Hill, Alton Barnes, Wiltshire. 8 August 1997. 264 ft (80 m) diameter at widest point; 204 circles. Wheat.

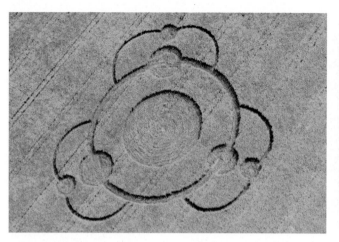

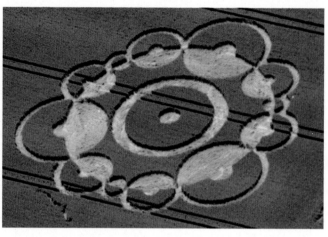

'Trefoil'. Goodworth Clatford, Hampshire. 10 May 1998. Approx. 140 ft (42 m) diameter ringed circle with three circles overlapping the ring at angles of approx. 120 degrees. Three outer half cardioids with circles at the top aligned above the first circles. Oilseed rape.

'Broach 1'. Clanfield, Hampshire. 22 June 1998. *c*.120 ft (36 m) overall. Wheat.

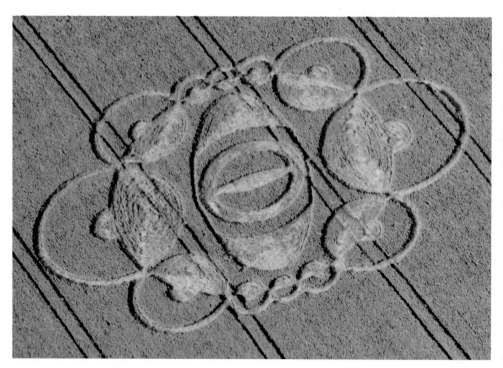

'Rose'. Fareham, Hampshire. 9 July 1998. *c*.240 ft (73 m) diameter. Wheat.

'Broach 2'. Windmill Hill, Butser, Hampshire. 10 July 1998. *c*.200 ft (61 m) diameter. Complex rectangular formation. Barley.

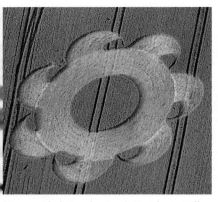

'Seven-sided Circular Saw'. Danebury Hill, Hampshire. 8 July 1998. *c.*130 ft (39 m) diameter. Wheat.

'Thought Bubble and Broach'. Danebury, Hampshire. 2 August 1998. *c.*60 ft (18 m) diameter. Wheat.

Danebury crescent, Hampshire. 2 August 1998. *c.*75 ft (23 m) diameter.

Three formations. Danebury Hill, Hampshire. 2 August 1998.

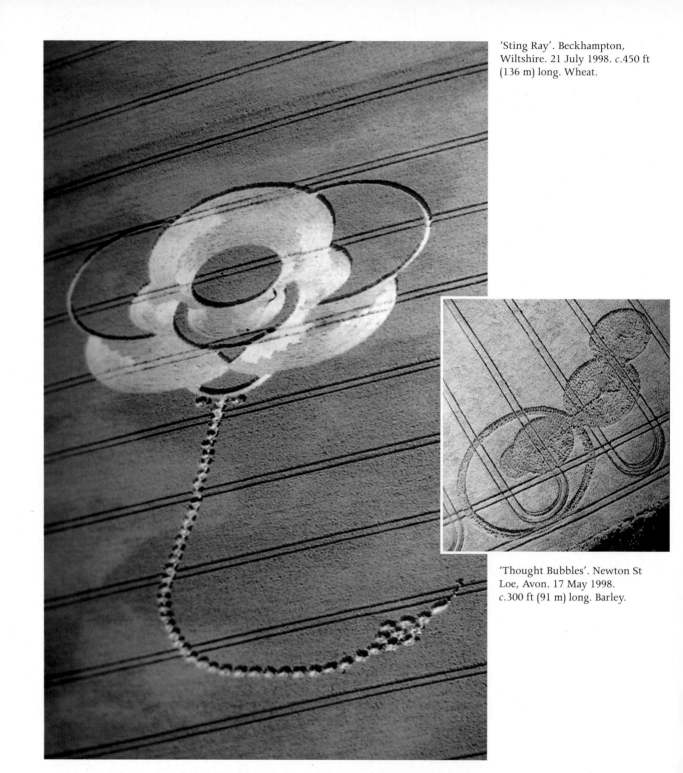

'Sting Ray'. Beckhampton, Wiltshire. 21 July 1998. *c.*450 ft (136 m) long. Wheat.

'Thought Bubbles'. Newton St Loe, Avon. 17 May 1998. *c.*300 ft (91 m) long. Barley.

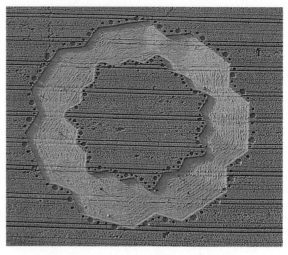

'Mandala'. Avebury Trusloe, Wiltshire. 20 June 1998.
c.200 ft (61 m) diameter. Wheat.

'Handkerchief with centre'. West Stowell, Wiltshire.
9 August 1998. c.500 ft (152 m) diameter. Wheat.

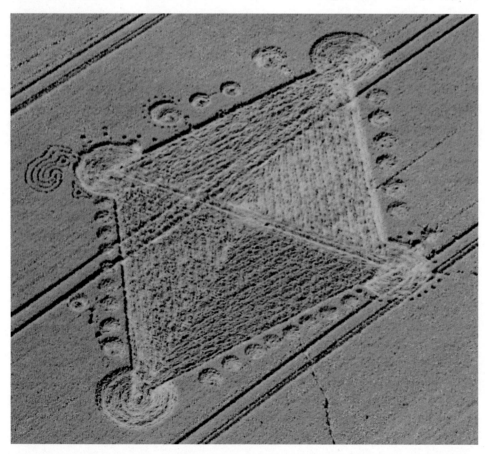

Elaborate rectangle.
Stanton St Bernard,
Wiltshire.
17 August 1998.
c.90 ft (27 m)
overall. Linseed.

'The Queen'. Lockeridge, Wiltshire. 6 August 1998. *c.*200 ft (61 m) overall. Wheat.

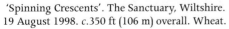
'Spinning Crescents'. The Sanctuary, Wiltshire.
19 August 1998. *c.*350 ft (106 m) overall. Wheat.

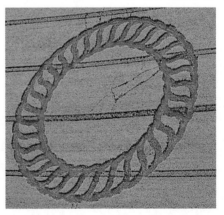

'Beltane Wheel'.
Silbury, Wiltshire.
14 May 1998. Approx.
250–280 ft (76–85 m)
diameter. Ringed
circle with standing
crop in the centre
and 33 scrolls
accurately fitted into
the ring. Formed
between 3 a.m. and
5 a.m. Oilseed rape.

vibrations to a much lesser degree. On the Tuesday she was fit and well, and again ate some of the grain she had brought with her from England. Within 15 minutes the same sensations returned, only to a more intense degree. She felt as though she was generating energy and wondered, quite seriously, 'if I might spontaneously combust'. It was then that she connected eating the grain with these symptoms.

She stopped eating the grain and went to work the following day, feeling much better. Barbara is a jeweller and works a great deal with electrical equipment, all of which shorted that day as soon as she got close to it. She gave some of the grain to her colleagues, all of whom, apparently, also experienced the effects as if they had ingested 'speed'.

After about five days Barbara returned to normal. She experimented eating the grain several times until there was no reaction – five or six weeks after Barbara left England. Had the grain lost its potency or had Barbara and her colleages become accustomed to it?

Barbara remarked that the 'energy' created seemed to have a healing quality, as evidenced when she was able to ease other people's pain by placing her hands on their pain spots.

A short while after the grain-eating experience, Barbara noticed that a wart appeared on her body. It was a common wart, but grew from a tiny spot (about a quarter of an inch (0.5cm) in diameter) to half an inch (1cm) high at the time of its subsequent removal, about six weeks after Barbara first noticed it. There is absolutely no evidence to suggest that the wart was in any way related to eating the grain, but Barbara feels it was directly connected.

The effects that Barbara felt after her grain-eating experience were:

Figure 42: Large circle, 'Hand of Friendship', Cherhill, near Calne, Wiltshire, 7 August 1993. Wheat

- deep, total body vibrations
- a core of extreme heat in the solar plexus
- a feeling of energy pouring out of her hands and the top of her head
- sleeplessness
- loss of appetite
- disorientation and inability to function effectively
- nervousness
- fluttering in the stomach.

As a footnote to this story, while I was gathering crop and seed samples for a photography research project, I had many samples left over and agreed to send some to Barbara in the States. Barbara reported: 'I did eat a little of the wheat sent to me, but experienced nothing.' What Barbara did not know was that the samples I provided had come from the 'control' samples taken from outside the crop formation.

The Missing Buckle

Another curious story with no apparent explanation concerns Bridget Engledow (who died in 1998). Bridget had visited the Cherhill formation, which lay in a field below the White Horse carved into the towering chalk hillside. The horse, although influenced by the ancient Uffington white horse, was in fact only cut in 1780, under the direction of a Dr Christopher Alsopp. Here she had stood at the perimeter of the largest circle.

On returning home from Cherhill, as Bridget was getting out of the car, her watch dropped off. The buckle was missing, but the stitching around the flap where the buckle was held was not damaged. How on earth had the buckle been lost from an undamaged strap? The buckle was never found.

Four days later Bridget visited the circle at the East Kennett crossroads with the friend.

She did not get out of the car. When she turned off

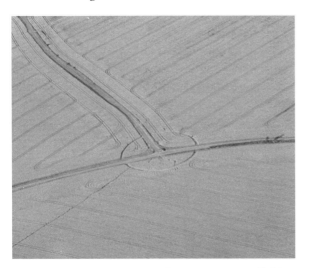

Figure 43: East Kennett Crossroads, West Overton, Wiltshire, 10 July 1993. Wheat

the car engine on her return home, her watch fell off again, her replacement strap cleanly sliced through. Both straps were leather and under a year old. She was not wearing anything sharp, nor was there anything sharp inside the car that could have been the cause.

Remote Audible Effects

The audible effects of circles are many and varied, and are heard not only whilst inside crop formations, but also in situations connected with the phenomenon any manner of miles away.

I am told that there are a number of 'inner' sounds – sounds associated with a quiet, 'meditative' state of mind (i.e., in a state of raised consciousness or awareness). Among these sounds are the trilling and ticking so often reported by those who have visited crop circles. I have experienced ticking not only in crop circles but also at home and, even more dramatically, during a meditation period at a Healing Centre at Shere, after giving a talk that morning.

One afternoon there, we all decided to do a meditation using a slide of the Dancing Man formation at Micheldever Station as our focal point.

After looking at the slide for a few minutes I closed my eyes, but to my annoyance found that my inner 'silence' was being disturbed by the ticking of a clock in the corner of the room. I resolved to try and rise above earthly distractions and concentrate on the spiritual. After a short time I was able to exclude the noise.

In the discussion following the meditation, two people remarked how irritated they had been by the ticking of the clock. 'Yes, the one in the corner,' I remarked. But there was no clock in the corner, and there was no clock in the passageway. In fact, there was no clock in the vicinity! There were over 100 people in the room and 13 of us heard the ticking.

I told this story at another talk and a woman rushed up afterwards to tell me that she had recently been praying in the same Sanctuary and had also heard the ticking. The noise had lasted about 20 minutes.

Another strange thing happened that day at Shere. After I had given my talk, several people came up to

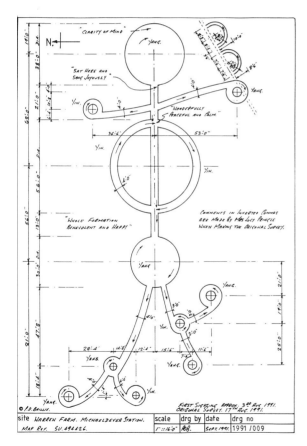

Figure 44: The 'Dancing Man', Micheldever, Hampshire, 2 August 1991. Wheat. © Peter Baillie

me afterwards saying that they had, for no explicable reason, 'fallen asleep' as I was showing slides of the more elaborate formations. This sort of thing had happened to me before and, being new to speaking in those days, had thoroughly unnerved me. However, what I had started to suspect soon became apparent as several other people joined our group and started discussing different aspects of my talk. The people who thought they had been asleep had, in fact, heard everything!

Many of the crop circle shapes resemble mandalas, traditionally used in meditation, and so could have induced a meditative state in some of the listeners. Or are these agroglyphs emitting harmonic vibrations, stimulating a part of the brain into a meditative state?

More Audible Effects

James Millen had a fascinating experience. In 1991 both he and his wife visited the Sceptre formation in the now-famous East Field at Alton Barnes. He recalls that the air was heavy and the crop was not moving. His wife had gone ahead to the formation. As James went to join her, he heard a rustling sound in the corn around him. When he stopped to listen, the rustling also stopped. He checked several times on his way down to the formation to make sure that 'I was not touching the corn on either side and looking to see if there were any rabbits, game birds or other animals.'

When he reached his wife he was surprised to hear her say that she had been 'worried by the rustling sound that had followed her down to the formation'. They had both found this puzzling. The noise did not occur as they made their way out of the field.

The following year, as they were walking along the path up to West Kennett long barrow, they both

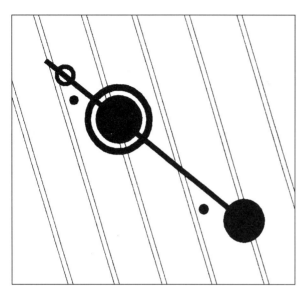

Figure 45: The 'Sceptre', East Field, Alton Barnes, Wiltshire, July 1991. © Nigel Tomsett and Debbie Pardoe

Remote Visual Effects

Ray Barnes witnessed a crop circle being formed in 1981 whilst out walking his dog (*see Chapter 1, pages 5–6*). Ray was 45 years old at the time of the sighting and, although he admits that an ensuing blindness could be coincidental, in his heart he believes there must be some connection with this incident. By early 1982, he realized there was something wrong with his right eye, and by May 1985 he had a fully developed cataract. The vision in his left eye also deteriorated over a period of two years. The cause of Ray's cataracts was unknown and his consultant ophthalmologist said that he had never come across a case of 'fluorescent sclera' (which is sometimes evidence of radiation exposure), before.

Ray underwent successful lens implant surgery in 1985 and 1987, and now his eyes are just about perfect. However, he recalls a dream so strange that the memory of the incident and its consequences has not faded.

'About two weeks before the first operation, I dreamt that I was put aboard an aircraft just prior to being operated on. The roof of the fuselage was painted green above me as I was wheeled along on the trolley. When my eye was uncovered after the operation the first thing I saw was a stainless steel ward trolley and apparently blue "electric" flames were licking along the steel tubes.

'After my operation had actually occurred, and my eye was uncovered, the first thing I saw was a stainless steel trolley and "electric" flames were, indeed, licking along it. This extreme sensitivity of vision lasted about three weeks, then disappeared quite suddenly.

noticed clicking noises 'that seemed to be in the air all around us'. A group of people on their way back from the barrow were coming towards them. As they passed James asked them if they had any idea what might be causing this noise. It seemed that the group had only become aware of the noise as they neared James and his wife. They found this strange, could offer no explanation and promptly hurried away.

James says that the clicking sound 'seemed to be jumping around in the air and was quite unlike anything I have heard'. At the time James did not connect it with the crop formation visible from the top of the barrow. A few days later his wife and sister found that they had recorded 'a cloud column coming right down to the glyph, with small white dots in attendance' on five of the photographs they had taken that day.

'During this period I could read a book in a totally darkened room at night. Halos and auras appeared round most things and in all movements of material I could detect moiré patterns such as you get in satins and silks. This temporary supervision was an enhancing experience and I was a bit sad when it ended.

'When I had my second operation, I was conscious when I was taken to the operating theatre. The roof of the annexe leading to theatre was just like the inside of the aircraft fuselage and painted the same green as my dream. Sadly the "extra" vision was not so pronounced this time and went after a period of a few days.'

Ray wonders if the duration of the 'special' sight was connected to the fact that his right eye (operated on first) was blind for longer than the left one.

SYNCHRONICITY

Synchronicity, or the phenomenon of things existing or occurring at the same time but in different places, seems to be on the increase. More and more people are experiencing strange synchronistic happenings. Is synchronicity itself becoming synchronistic? Jung calls it an 'Acausal Connecting Principle'. There is no doubt that there is increasing evidence of interaction between people, much of which I am sure goes unnoticed.

A Case of Synchronicity
At about 11.15 p.m. one August evening in 1993, Kobus Nieuwmeiser went into the single Crescent formation at Tawsmead Copse in the vicinity of Alton Barnes. He had decided to sleep in the formation, something he had done in other formations in previous years. He was in the formation for a period of five hours. While in the Crescent he felt 'captive', unable to move for approximately two hours. During this time he experienced constant visual enhancement, which manifested itself as a sparkling effect in the surrounding crop. He also suffered a humming sound in his ears.

The lights at a nearby farm went out at 1 a.m. At 2.30 a.m. a mist engulfed the whole area and, even though it was quite cold, Kobus remembers that his body remained warm. At 3.30 a.m. he observed a luminous, cylindrical shape (lying horizontally in the

Figure 46: Crescent at Tawsmead Copse, West Stowell, Wiltshire, July 1992. Wheat. © Grant Wakefield

sky), looming about 330 feet (100m) away in the direction of Draycott. The segmented object moved backwards and forwards for approximately 10 minutes. It then separated off in all directions, only to reassemble again. After a further 10 minutes, it finally disappeared down the field.

At 3.35 a.m. Kobus's girlfriend Lauren, in Oxford, was woken by a metallic humming sound and strange surreal images in her head. She felt completely paralysed.

Here we have yet another example of a strange interaction between a crop formation and two or more people (*see pages 41–3 in Chapter 3*). Throughout history we have had well-documented cases of ESP. Could the crop formations be acting as facilitators? It would seem that Lauren, many miles away in Oxford, was sharing Kobus's experience in Wiltshire. Did some 'intelligence' plant the identical experience in Lauren or was Lauren 'receiving' the experience from Kobus? Maybe it is nothing more than coincidence.

Kobus and Lauren both quite independently told me that they had been paralysed and unable to move. Lauren had found this rather frightening, for she discovered that she was unable to call out to her flatmate who had received a telephone call at the time the paralysis occurred. Kobus, on the other hand, was not alarmed. In fact, being a fidgety person by nature, he rather relished this unusual state of immobility! He had intended to visit another formation nearby, but had to shelve the idea when he found he was unable to move. He decided to 'go with the flow' and simply observe what was happening to him. His body was rigid.

The reported visual disturbance effect reported by Kobus is a strange and unmistakable connection between his experience and that of Ralph Noyes three years previously in the Triangle formation in Beckhampton (*see pages 40–1*).

Sleep Paralysis

Shirley Gifford had a similar experience to Lauren's feeling of paralysis while in bed.

'I heard the telephone ringing (which is right by the bed). I tried so hard to wake up or to come back, but to no avail. I knew who was phoning [and this was later confirmed].

'I felt apprehensive the first time it happened, wondering why I was unable to wake up and answer the phone when I was able to hear it ringing. The second time it happened was exactly the same; the phone was ringing, and I said to myself within the dream: "Don't worry, they will phone again when I get back."'

It is very possible that these experiences of paralysis are linked to the sleep-related disturbance of sleep paralysis. I have experienced this myself and it can be extremely frightening. It is a relatively common phenomenon which usually occurs at the time when people are just going to sleep or are waking up, and is due to the body deliberately inducing paralysis during deep REM sleep to prevent us from physically acting out our dreams. It causes muscle paralysis and other frightening sensations such as choking. However, in the case of Kobus and Lauren this would seem unlikely, as they both suffered paralysis simultaneously. This would tend to invite speculation that some additional cause was present.

The Westbury Murders and Other Events

Ray Barnes lives in the small town of Westbury in Wiltshire which, according to dowsers, lies on a massive negative energy line, and which has been at the heart of the crop circle phenomenon. Ray has been most generous with his time in recounting various experiences (*see Chapter 1, and above*). On one occasion I had telephoned him to obtain yet more information. The conversation was almost complete when he suddenly said: 'You know the murders have started again, don't you?' What a way to stop a conversation!

A succession of particularly gruesome attacks and murders had taken place in Westbury, which has a population of only 10,000, since 1984. The grim toll read as follows:

- In 1984, a petrol attendant was shot and disabled in a bungled robbery.
- In 1986, a stable girl was disfigured for life after an acid attack organized by an ex-boyfriend.
- Also in 1986, a maths teacher who had a jealous obsession with a local man, used an axe to murder the man's wife and eight-month-old daughter.
- In 1987 Michael Ryan visited Westbury and bought the selection of guns he used in the Hungerford Massacre, 40 miles away, from the gun shop in Edward Street.
- In 1989 another local man abducted and murdered his former girlfriend.
- In 1990, a man was found hanged in the house he shared with his lover, whose mutilated body had been found earlier.
- In 1992 there were more grisly happenings: a young mother of three was killed and her charred body

found in the woods – a local man was charged with the murder; a man was accused of the attempted murder of his ex-girlfriend and her male friend by slitting their throats; and two men were charged with wounding a man in the throat with a high-powered air rifle when trying to collect a debt.

A month after this astonishing telephone call I visited Ray Barnes in his cycle shop in Westbury.

'You wrote the article in the *Independent*, didn't you?' he asked.

'What article?' I replied.

'The one describing the murders I was telling you about. The article came out two weeks after I spoke to you.'

I had written no such article for the *Independent*. Yet another case of synchronicity!

Ray runs a most efficient and thriving cycle shop, yet strange things start to happen at the beginning of May each year; not just in his shop but, according to his sales reps, in most shops in the south of England.

Synchronicity manifests itself in unusual buying patterns. For example, several customers will come in asking for the same part one after the other. It often happens that the part may not have been sold for several years, then Ray will sell three, four, five, even six of them in less than half an hour. This pattern will repeat and repeat until it reaches a peak in July, and then stops. It happens too regularly to be just coincidence.

One specific example of this occurred in May 1992. Ray normally keeps in stock only a couple of 500A tyres, as they are rare and demand is small. Not only did he sell all his stock inside an hour, but he also took orders for another five!

Chapter Five

Other Levels of Consciousness

As we saw in Chapter 3, the different frequencies of brain waves are associated with different states of consciousness. Emotional shock seems to cause a relapse to Theta waves from the normal pattern of Beta and Alpha rhythms, with a consequent loss of higher brain functions and logic (i.e., arithmetical ability), which are replaced with irrational fears, visions, day-dreaming and loss of time sense. Though this state is usual for children up to the age of eight or nine years, it tends to be unpleasant for adults, as it can release sub-conscious material, some of which can be traumatic. On a more positive note a Theta state may enable self-healing to take place as tensions imposed by higher mental stress can be released.

Do we operate on different levels of consciousness? I suspect that we do and that most of us are unaware of doing so. The stories in this chapter give me reason to believe that we are experiencing these other levels more often than we realize. It seems that the reported instances of loss of time, suspension of thought, inability to move, 'enchantment' and geological distortions all fall within this same category of a possible shift into another overlapping dimension of consciousness. There is evidence of this sort of thing happening both in certain crop circles, and in places of sacred antiquity.

COUNTING PROBLEMS

One of the classic ways in which this altered consciousness is demonstrated is an inability to count! While drawing a sketch map of a line of trees within a 'captured' circle, Michael Newark was unable to count beyond six or seven trees, as 'the patterns seemed wrong'. As soon as he left the circle he had no problem whatsoever. Thinking this strange, he repeated the exercise twice: each time he was inside the circle he suffered the same counting problem, but when he was outside the circle he had no trouble at all.

What strange influence inside the circle had affected Michael? There is a belief that when we enter an ancient circle of trees or stone, we have embarked on a sacred journey into other times and space. We have entered a place of mystery and enchantment and are not there for the purpose of counting each individual stone, but to accept the creation as a whole, enhancing our awakened understanding and bringing us new levels of insight.

It would seem that many people experience a similar sense of 'disorientation' while visiting crop formations, which may linger for a varying length of time afterwards. Nancy Talbot, an American researcher who has visited crop formations for the past six or seven years, has a strangely similar story to tell. Nancy had agreed to help two friends by printing up a batch of T-shirts in the States, for them to sell on lecture tours.

'After getting the shirts printed a weird thing started to happen. Every time I was called on to do this I found I could not count the wretched things, no matter how careful I was. For the record I've been producing major outdoor musical festivals in the US for 15 years and at these shows I have sold 10,000–15,000 shirts per show. Truck loads. I never had a problem counting them. And with my friends' shirts I couldn't count up to 50 accurately. This went on until I finally sent them all off, and I hope I never have to count them again.'

Nancy was in England during the summer of 1993

and continues her tale.

'I was completely disorientated again in the work I was supposed to be doing. I couldn't stay on track for even a day. And, remember, I run shows which draw 20,000–30,000 people. I build whole cities on farms out in the country to house these people, providing water, electricity, food, a road system, not to mention the shows themselves – tents, buildings and so on – all with no trouble at all. But I get out in the crop circle fields of England and I can't tie my shoelaces.

'It doesn't make sense that I can manage all the details of a US$500,000 show lasting a week or more, but I can't keep my mind focused for even a day in England. It's weird. I felt like it the whole time I was here in 1993. I really felt like a jerk actually, or like I was losing my mind or something.'

There have been suggestions that this type of effect could be due to low frequency waves caused by certain specific frequencies of microwave radiation. However, much work needs to be done in this area before we reach any firm conclusion.

TIME SLIPPAGES

Ray Barnes, several of whose experiences have already been recounted, keeps a journal, faithfully recording anything unusual.

On Tuesday 24 July 1990, Ray was out rather later than intended and was looking across the field where he had witnessed a crop circle form (*see pages 5–6*), when he noticed the shadows of the trees on the right

Figure 47: Ray Barnes overlooking the field where the events occurred

Figure 48a: The shadows converging. © Ray Barnes

Figure 48b: The shadows have returned to the parallel. © Ray Barnes

Figure 48c: The quadruple circle. © Ray Barnes

were converging towards the shadows of the trees on his left.

'The convergence was much sharper than could be accounted for by perspective and looked to be about 15 degrees [see Figure 48a]. The following evening I tried to photograph this convergence, but without success. However, I did note my own shadow standing next to the tree, which appeared to be wrong.

'When I stood ten feet to the right of the tree our shadows were parallel, and when I stood ten feet to the left of it there was a significant convergence.

'By Thursday evening my excitement was increasing. There was a heath fire somewhere to the west and the smoke from it was blowing across the field. The smoke was brown and so dense that I could not see the sky through it. But then something strange caught my attention. Half-way across the field it was if a glass "wall" had been erected. The smoke blew and billowed against the wall, but apparently could not cross it; to the left of the barrier the air was clear, and the sky and clouds could be seen.

'From Tuesday to Friday the weather was extremely hot and I had a curious feeling that the converging shadows or "time-slipping" effect presaged an imminent corn circle, but I was not sure how imminent.

'Sunday was cool and showery and, not being totally satisfied with the strange visual abnormalities, I decided to run a test using a pendulum and compass to measure the angle between the shadows. The shadows were exactly the same. Still not satisfied with the results, I ran further experiments. On Wednesday evening I took a one-mile (1.6km) detour to the far side of the field so that I could view the shadows from a distance. I was very disappointed to find that they were parallel [see Figure 48b], but then I noticed that a quadruple circle had formed [see Figure 48c]. I later discovered this happened between late Tuesday evening and early Wednesday morning. On Thursday it got very hot again and once more the shadows began to converge. I stopped two passers-by who agreed that the shadows "were not right". Having used a compass on the shadows and sun, and having taken a number of readings on both Thursday and Friday night, I found that there was a divergence of six degrees.

'I deliberately set up an experiment with a six-degree error, but found it difficult to believe that I could make such an error continually in a set of readings.

'At last I thought I had real evidence of a "time

slip", but when the shadows and sun line were plotted out, despite appearing to be visually reciprocal, they were not.'

Traced drawings of the photographs have been taken and superimposed over each other. The angle divergence would appear to be between 15 and 20 degrees.

Ray explained that the apparent time break did not stay in one place but, over the two weeks of observation, seemed to wander randomly over a 400-yard (364m) front. The 'glass wall' appeared to run parallel to, and about 200 yards (182m) from, an energy line identified by dowsing, and extended into the sky to an unknown height. Ray had watched the vapour trail of an airplane fracture where the 'wall'

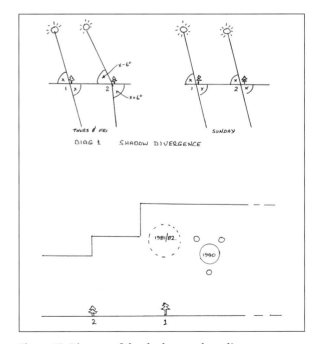

Figure 49: Diagram of the shadows and sun line.
© Ray Barnes

extended upwards. The plane was flying at around 25,000 feet (7,576m).

On another occasion, Ray was walking his dogs past the energy line, when his attention was drawn to a walnut tree in the hedge. He had not noticed a walnut tree there before, so went over to look at it. He thought it strange that a walnut should grow to the height the tree was. When he looked higher, he noticed that from approximately 15 to 20 feet (4.5–6m) up, the tree was a horse chestnut: there was no possibility of mistaking the single-fingered, dark green leaf of the walnut with the five-fingered leaf of the horse chestnut. The tree is now back to normal.

Ray's experiences of time slips have occurred over the years since he first witnessed a crop circle form. Just after that time he was standing at the White Horse at Westbury, looking at two circles which had formed on the fields towards Bratton.

'The smoke from two chimneys in the valley was blowing towards each other. Turning round to go home, I noticed that there were a lot of people standing around in groups, but they weren't moving or talking. They were like statues standing on the grass and I had walked 250 yards (227m) between them before they started to move and talk.'

Ray tells of another example when he was out walking his dogs one July evening.

'I took the dogs to the field where I had seen the first circle form. The field was being "combined" with two harvesters and I estimated that there was 20 minutes to go before the job was complete. I walked on for about ten feet, looked up and the job was done. How or why I don't know.'

It is interesting to note that Ray, like several other people who have sent me reports, frequently seems to lose periods of time ranging from a few minutes to a couple of hours.

Margaret Randall (*see pages 27–30*) consistently loses time whilst in crop circles, by about 75 per cent of real time. She experienced another strange effect while in the Ogbourne St George formation in August 1992, and for 40 minutes or so after leaving the circle – she found she was quite unable to think of anything nasty or unpleasant. This struck her as being particularly strange and to that end she redoubled her efforts, but to no avail. Perhaps she had entered a dimension of raised consciousness where, due to the fact that no evil existed in that dimension, she was unable to access anything bad.

Time Slips and Ancient Places

Time slips and other facets of altered levels of consciousness also occur at ancient stone circles and other sacred monuments, which are often precisely aligned with sun or moon on certain ancient festival days, such as Lammas – the harvest festival of the Great Earth Goddess – in late July/early August. Silbury Hill, near the Avebury Stone Circle, and the largest man-made hill in Europe at 522 feet (158m) in diameter and 130 feet (39m) high, is one such place.

It is a Late Neolithic/Early Bronze Age monument, around 4,500 years old. The hill is thought to have been named after King Zel, who is still reported riding around the hill on moonlight nights, dressed in golden armour.

Silbury Hill was constructed in three stages, with a complex anti-subsidence system in place. The hill was clearly built to last, and was obviously of great significance for the people who toiled to build it. Although there are no signs of the hill ever being used as a burial mound (despite the best efforts of various 18th- and 19th-century antiquarians to find any such evidence), we do know from the remains of winged ants found within it that it was constructed just after mid-summer, at the time of the Lammas festival.

In March 1993 I visited Silbury Hill with David Russell, an architect and archaeologist. We gasped in astonishment when we got there, for the hill was entirely surrounded by water.

The mound lies on an ephemeral spring that rises for almost six weeks every year in early spring. It was a truly awesome sight and we felt privileged to be witnesses to this relatively rare event. We set off on our climb at about 11 a.m., which, despite the size of the hill, is surprisingly easy. On reaching the summit the panoramic view spreading out beneath displayed the entire recumbent Mother Goddess figure in her full glory.

Individually we dowsed the 'right' spot on which to sit. The moment I sat down, I felt I had 'come

Figure 50: Silbury Hill, near Marlborough, Wiltshire

home'. I felt as though I was sinking lower and lower into the very bowels of the hill. I closed my eyes and decided to 'go with it'. No sounds of traffic intruded. The harmony with the hill was complete.

After what seemed like a short time I opened my eyes and David seemed to be stirring too. We made our way down and walked towards the nearby West Kennett Long Barrow. To try and bring myself back to reality I looked at my watch; it said 12.15 p.m. I shook it several times, but it still read 12.15 p.m. How could it be? We had only been on top of Silbury Hill for about 10 minutes and yet an hour and a quarter had passed.

Moreover, I can only sit crosslegged on the ground for 10 minutes at the most without getting up and moving my legs – and I know I had not done so. Nor was I stiff or numb when I stood up. David was just as surprised as I was, for apparently, despite arthritis in his knees which causes discomfort, he too had not needed to move his position.

DISORIENTATIONS

Feelings of disorientation and confusion upon entering crop formations are relatively common. Mrs X

Figure 51: Silbury Hill surrounded by water, March 1993

had a 'suspension of mind' while in the Upham Insectogram, near Bishops Waltham in Hampshire. Following directions I had driven Mrs X, a friend of hers and one of my neighbours to visit the formation one damp afternoon in early June 1991.

It was quite a long walk to the formation, but I left shortly after arriving, as I had a persistent feeling of distaste and unease. The others stayed in the formation some two hours while I waited in the car. Eventually they came out and I noticed that Mrs X, who is normally a bright, witty conversationalist, was very quiet. In fact she was silent. Her friend rang me later and mentioned that Mrs X had 'gone walkabout' and had not replied to any comments, nor been involved in any conversation, whilst in the circle.

Mrs X herself states that she felt rather suspended – that is, with her thinking processes suspended – yet focused on objectives of meeting further engagements that evening. (As a footnote, ten days later Mrs X telephoned me to say that she had had no energy since the visit. In fact the loss of energy continued and she felt that the visit triggered a total collapse of her energy system, which took six months to correct.) She has refused all my invitations to visit a crop circle since!

The Beckhampton Spiral was also responsible for much disorientation during 1995. I visited the formation with a friend, Keith Wakelam, a retired electronic engineer, and we had great difficulty in finding our way to the centre of the formation. When we did finally reach it, our compass oscillated wildly for some considerable time. Keith walked around the first spiral, dowsing the energies with rods. Every 45 degrees, the rods changed polarity, which seemed to indicate some sort of dynamo effect – an alternating negative/positive energy.

Both of us felt very unwell in the formation, suffering severe migraines, and had great difficulty in gathering plant samples and conducting further research. We eventually got back to the car, and sat for a while waiting for the migraine effects to subside. When Keith drove off it was several minutes before either of us realized that he was happily driving on the wrong side of the road (the rather busy A40!), and even after that, we twice got lost getting home, on a road that is very familiar to both of us!

Losses of Memory

In 1993 five crop formations appeared in a line stretching from Wanborough in Surrey to the outskirts of Guildford. The ancient Saxon name for Wanborough was 'Wenberge', or 'bump-barrow' – probably referring to the nearby Bronze Age bell bar-

Figure 52: St Bartholomew, Wanborough. © Charles Bone, PPRI, ARCA. Painting on card

Figure 53: Christopher Weeks drawing the Wanborough satellite, 1993

row on the Hog's Back chalk ridge which runs through the area.

The second formation to appear at Wanborough was the Crescent or Yin/Yang symbol. Surrey researcher Christopher Weeks had gone to this formation with the express intention of taking photographs. But when he went into the circle he simply could not think why he was there! He came out of the formation and remembered his purpose; on entering for the second time he yet again completely forgot the reason for his visit. This happened four times before he managed to take any photographs! He is not a 'dozy' fellow!

Worse was to follow. As part of a homoeopathic and healing experiment, I buried four bottles of water inside this formation and two control bottles

outside, making careful, comprehensive and exact notes to assist me with my dowsing when I came to locate them later. Two weeks later Christopher Weeks and I met to collect the bottles from the formation. I found the control bottles with ease, but simply could not locate the ones inside. We had to stop before we dug up the whole field!

Being of a resolute nature Christopher refused to be beaten and, knowing the problems he had experienced when trying to take photographs in this formation, resolved to use 'lateral' thinking to solve my problem. Ten minutes later he had reclaimed all four bottles. They had been nowhere near the written directions I had so carefully logged in my book. If I lived my life in this disorientated fashion I would be going backwards fast!

More Confusion

Christopher Weeks again experienced a strange occurrence in the Medusa formation overlooking Avebury. He and a friend were the first people into the formation on the morning of 28 June 1993. He was standing in the formation when suddenly his eyes went out of focus and a thin white mist appeared. When the mist lifted and his eyes returned to normal, he could see three box shapes in the corn which had not been there previously. Confused, he went to join his companion and asked whether he had seen any boxes in the formation? His friend said no, and that he must be imagining things. After lunch, they went back to the circle and there were the three boxes Christopher had seen earlier.

This formation had another curious effect on Christopher. In one particular spot he found himself overcome with sadness and close to tears.

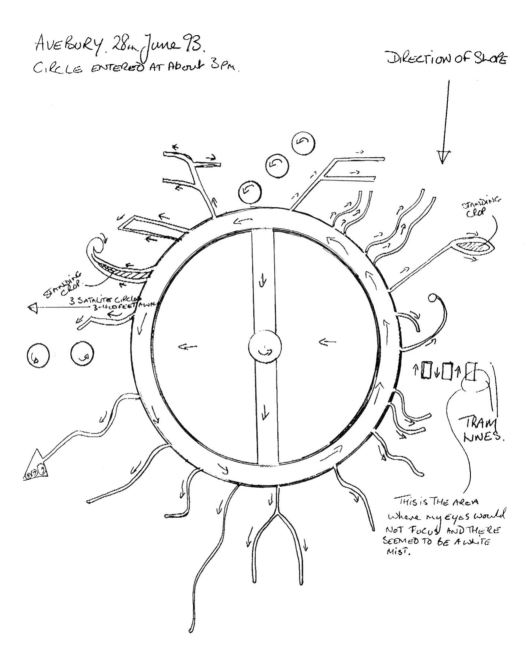

AVEBURY. 28th June 93.
CIRCLE ENTERED AT ABOUT 3PM.

DIRECTION OF SLOPE

STANDING CROP

STANDING CROP

3 SATALITE CIRCLES 3-4.00 FEET AWAY

TRAM LINES.

THIS IS THE AREA WHERE MY EYES WOULD NOT FOCUS AND THERE SEEMED TO BE A WHITE MIST.

Figure 54: 'Medusa', Avebury, Wiltshire, 1 July 1993. Wheat. © Christopher Weeks

A Feeling of Déjà Vu

In 1993, Nancy Talbot had promised to collect plant specimens for Dr Levengood, the American bio-physicist responsible for pioneering research on the effects formations have on plants, and who is coming up with some intriguing results.

The previous day she had experienced a strange sense of déjà vu, and had told Canadian Chad Deetken and others that an addition to the existing formation at East Kennett was going to take place that night.

She suggested they station themselves at Overton Hill in order to witness this happening. At the time she could not think why on earth she had said this and, indeed, felt rather pompous making the statement. Then, when the addition occurred the next day, she was astonished, despite having been so confident the day before.

Chad Deetken and a colleague did indeed go up to Overton Hill, as suggested, but left about 2.30 a.m. While they were there they observed a strange white mist, in the shape of a horse, heading across the field towards the West Kennett Long Barrow sometime after midnight.

Figure 55: The 'Adam and Eve' stones at the Avebury complex, Wiltshire. These outlying stones are said to disappear mysteriously if you are not meant to see them

Time Travelling?

Avebury is another site often thought of as a 'magical' and 'mystical' place, and many people have experienced its curious effects. Music has often been heard coming from the Avebury stone complex, and lights are seen dancing around the stones. People have also reported seeing small figures moving among the stones. The stone circle used to host a fair regularly within its boundaries, as the logical open meeting place for miles around.

A friend, who had been brought up in the Middle East, was sitting by the Standing Stones in the Cove at Avebury one day. She began to describe the scene she saw in front of her. She described a small settlement of houses with open-topped roofs from which smoke was rising. The inhabitants were small and the women were dressed in long skirts, the men in tunic-like garments. The children ran around barefoot playing with the animals. There was a queue of darker-skinned people outside one of the houses, which had bunches of dried herbs hanging against

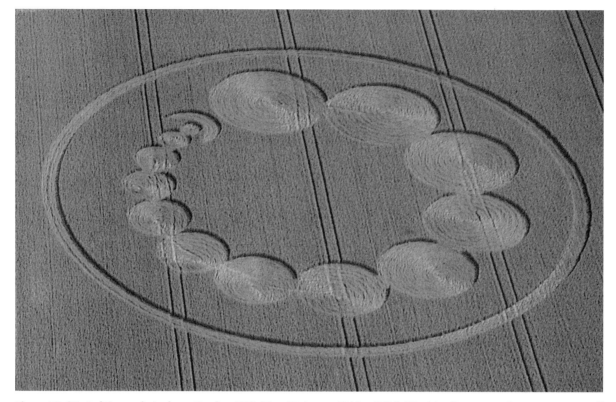

Figure 56: 'Nested Dragon', Avebury Trusloe, Wiltshire, 15 August 1994, *c.*150 ft (45m) in diameter. Wheat. © Ron Russell

the wall. It appeared as though these people had travelled from afar. As they came out of the house they were each carrying a little leather pouch. Did this contain herbal remedies, I wonder? Had my friend been able to travel back to ancient times when Avebury was a healing centre?

Ron Russell, an American artist deeply interested in crop circles, had a similar experience of a time slip at the Nested Dragon formation at Avebury Trusloe, in August 1994. He and a friend, John, went into the circle at around 11.30 p.m., on the day of its creation. After taking a roll of film, Ron left John in the circle

to go back to their car for some more film.

'I retraced our path toward the edge of the field and I walked and walked and walked but I never found the edge of the field and I became concerned as so much time was passing. I trudged onward knowing the the edge was near (it must be, surely) and the grass grew shorter and the tramlines disappeared and I found myself in a state of disbelief. I looked hard every which way and spotted some flickering lights in the distance which I trudged toward, sweating as a result of this long walk which I estimated to have been about 30 minutes.

'As I approached the flickering lights and some intervening bushes I could see they were fires. I stopped in my tracks and thought to myself, "They don't have open fires in Avebury Trusloe at this time of night. What has happened to me? Have I gone into some sort of dimensional shift here? And what about the tramlines disappearing? And the air becoming somehow thicker?"

'I slowly walked closer to the bushes and I could clearly see on the other side there were two bonfires and several short people milling about them in a sort of a little clearing surrounded by several thatched huts. "What a great opportunity!" I thought and as I was about to approach this scene the thought of being burned at the stake flashed through my mind and I paused to consider this. "What if I have slipped over to the fifteenth century?" I asked myself. "This was not a very open period in men's thoughts and beliefs and with my clothing and mannerisms and cameras slung around my neck (without film!), I doubt if I would be invited to dinner."

'Slowly I backtracked to get John. I followed my tracks through the short wheat and finally came to the faint beginnings of the tramline I had come down. I followed this for about 30 minutes and at last found my way back into the formation where John was standing.

'"Come with me, John!" I exclaimed, "I have found a time door!", and we proceeded back the way I had just come, except that we came right away to the edge of the field and the car! As I explained all this to him and apologized for my long absence, which I calculated at over an hour (I did not have my watch on), he looked at me in a bemused way and said, "Ron, you've only been gone five minutes!" I was stunned and thought he was jesting with me and went over all the details again.

'We could never locate the encampment with the fire. Was I delusional? I thought not but am at a loss to explain this further.'

STATES OF CONSIOUSNESS

How aware are we of the different states of mind? We know that different areas of the brain have different roles to play in the way our minds function. It has been proved by the late Maxwell-Cade (in *The Awakening Mind*) and others who have continued his research, that it is possible to control our superficial blood flow, thereby adjusting our body and mind accordingly.

In order to achieve higher states of consciousness, several well-tested techniques can be used, demonstrating the potential control we have over our minds and bodies. Yogis, for example have developed this skill to such a degree that they can control their blood flow, reducing the action of their body organs, and thereby enter a state of near hibernation for prolonged periods.

Maxwell-Cade identified 'a hierarchy of levels of consciousness'. He described them as:

sleeping (including the hypnagogic and hypnopompic states); waking; the relaxation response and meditation; the fourth state in which continuous self-awareness is maintained in addition to awareness of the external environment – which we call the Awakened Mind. For the sixth, seventh and eighth states, there are as many terms as there are philosophers and writers on the subject, and in order to arrive at those that are inclusive yet illustrative enough to be informative, we have chosen to call them, respectively, creativity and psychedelia, which means mind-creating, and cosmic consciousness.

Maxwell-Cade's levels seem to correspond largely with those described by Carl Jung. He saw the sixth state as the condition of Jung's Collective Unconscious, the Group Mind, and therefore likened Jung's Group Consciousness or Collective Unconscious to the fifth state, as being 'the prime area of higher creative development'.

TWO STRANGE INCIDENTS

The final two stories in this chapter are located near a renowned beauty spot in Hampshire – Cheesefoot Head – an area at the heart of the crop circle phenomenon.

It is not unusual for people to be reluctant to commit their experiences to paper. Sometimes, the effect of the experience is so profound that they simply cannot bear to relive it. The couple who related this story (and who wish to remain anonymous) felt exactly this way about recording what happened to them, and it took two years before they eventually felt ready to pass on the details.

One July evening in 1990 they decided to go for a walk at the vast natural amphitheatre of Cheesefoot Head, which is overlooked by the A272 Petersfield to Winchester Road.

'It was a beautiful evening, warm and sunny and mellow, when we arrived at the car park. We thought that the views from this high spot were magnificent, and in the clear evening light we noticed that you could see other high points many miles away, west and east. We commented that at one time it may have been used as a beacon hill, part of a chain leading into Wessex.

'We have little knowledge of ley lines, but we felt that this would be a powerful place for these lines because of its height, its clear views for miles around and its large areas of unspoilt surrounding countryside. We felt that there was a type of energy there, but I must emphasize that we had gone to Cheesefoot Head with no preconceived ideas other than it would be a nice place for a walk. We left the car park and walked north on the footpath. Falling away to our left was lower ground (the amphitheatre) and we were surprised to see a crop circle there. It may have been in the local newspaper (although we were unaware of this) because a few people had stopped their cars on the A272 and were viewing it from the roadside.

'We talked about the mystery surrounding crop circles and continued along the footpath, which was fenced on the left with a small bank rising on the right. We wondered if crop circles came where ley lines met. The footpath led into a wood on our right, still fenced on the left, with the crop circles now behind us on the left.

'The wood had a strange atmosphere, quite dark and still with an air of heaviness and watchfulness. We have felt this in woods before, noticing the difference between walking in beech woods and walking among conifers. However, this watchfulness made us feel uneasy. My husband needed to "spend a penny" and I found myself saying strangely: "Not in here; it is forbidden." We felt extremely uneasy and we were very relieved when the footpath led us out of the wood into open farmland.

'We had not seen anyone on the footpath ahead of us, nor were we aware of anyone following behind. We were grateful for the solitude to enjoy the summer evening and we felt better now we were out of the wood and dismissed our apprehensions as overactive imagination.

'We continued north along the footpath, which had widened into a cart track. It was no longer fenced to the left but was bordered by a cornfield, with a low hedge on our right, less than four feet [1.2m] in height, with a field behind it. The cart track led us downhill to a second wood.

'We had not gone far into this when we felt ill at ease again, and suddenly heard very loud and rather menacing laughter not too far ahead. The laughter was so loud it had an unnatural ring. It had a physical quality. The cart track we were following was like a broad swathe through the wood. We couldn't see anybody, nor had we been aware of anyone in front of us. We both suddenly felt afraid and my husband said: "We are turning back!"

'Despite having looked forward to this walk in a new and beautiful area (and I am always one who likes to know what is around the corner), I didn't argue. We turned back on our tracks at once, with a sense of fear.

'We were now backtracking, going uphill heading south, with the small hedge on our left and the cornfield on our right. It was still light. All the while, we kept looking over our shoulders at the wood that we had just left, but no one ever came out of it.

'Then we became aware of loud rustling noises keeping pace with us behind the hedge to our left. We could see nothing. The noises stopped when we stopped, and began again as we proceeded. We did this on purpose as a "test"; we still had a strong feeling of being watched, of being followed.

'We were fearful, but kept the knot of fear under control by expressing our concern to each other in a light manner, and we hurried greatly. When we talked about it afterwards we had both felt that we were afraid to express our fear as if in doing so, we would have been lost.

'We were startled even further when a short distance ahead of us, a stag seemed to come from nowhere and suddenly burst through a gap across our path, across the cornfield on our right and disappeared into a wood on the far side of the cornfield. We stood still in amazement and agreed that it couldn't have been behind the low hedge, as we would have seen it. It was very frightened; we stood and stared while it fled across the field. But it definitely wasn't the stag making the noises because they began again as we continued.

'Fear now lay heavy in our stomachs; we had to face the first wood we had come through, where we had felt so uneasy and "watched". There was no other route, and dusk was falling.

'Again, we didn't express our fears too much because we were afraid to do so – as if fear would create fear and whatever this horrible thing was, would grow with it, feed on it.

'We just said to each other that we did not want to go through the wood, but we would talk loudly about anything light – matter-of-fact, day-to-day things. I was so afraid and when we compared notes later we both felt the same.

'We entered the wood and the footpath was so narrow, we could only walk in single file. The noises that had been following us all the way along the cart track behind the hedge, now came with us into the wood. The noises were about three to four feet [a metre or so] to our left and kept pace with us, moving in a straight line. There was no close undergrowth – in fact, I remember it as being almost bare under the trees – and our view was not obscured in any way, yet we could see nothing of what we were constantly hearing. It was only self-control that prevented me from panicking. Again, giving-in would mean succumbing to this horrible sense of being watched, and the noises caused by an unseen presence that definitely did not want us there; it seemed we were being hurried away in no uncertain terms. Apart from the noises of whatever was keeping pace with us through the woods, the place felt quite still. The strong sense of watchfulness, of a presence, a most unpleasant presence – malevolent – remained.

'We pretended that everything was all right and went through the wood as quickly as possible without actually running. As we came out the other side of the wood we said: "Thank goodness that's over!" But it wasn't. At that moment I was overwhelmed by a heavy feeling all over me and had strong sensations almost like electric shocks throughout my body. The rustling noises continued a few feet away along the grassy bank, keeping an even pace and straight line.

'I just managed to keep control and continued praying silently, putting protection around us. I felt that it was a matter of exerting my will over this presence that was invading me with these awful sensations. I remember saying that it was not all over and then we ran like fury, up the remains of the foothpath, back to the car park, into the car. We sped away, not stopping until we reached the village of Southwick, about 25 miles [40 km] away.

'While we were driving (very fast, to put the place behind us as quickly as possible), we said that we wouldn't talk about it in the car. Afterwards, we agreed that this was because we felt as if there was still a presence in the car – we still felt we were being "watched".

'We stopped at a pub and talked about what had happened. Apart from the actual happenings and the intense fear, we felt that for some reason we had been sensitive to certain energies. We were not wanted where we had been and were guided away in the manner described.

'We had seen no one else on the walk apart from those who had viewed the crop circles from the main road. We had just gone there for a walk, not knowing what the place would be like, no preconceived ideas, and not knowing the crop circles were there. On returning home, my parents (who had been babysitting for us) could see we were upset, but we were unable to tell them what had happened as we were still afraid and felt that talking about it then would bring "it" into the house.

'We had agreed in the pub not to discuss it after leaving the pub unless we discussed it in the open air. When we did eventually tell my parents, they were very aware of our fear and they have never forgotten it.

'I wondered if we might return in the future and explore the area south of the A272 where there were further magnificent views, but that night I dreamed of rams' heads on poles by the roadside at Cheesefoot Head. I took that as a further warning, and we shall never return. Since then we have purposely avoided the road that would take us past Cheesefoot Head, and we have only travelled once along part of it since and then only as far as Hinton Ampner [about three miles (4.8km) from Cheesefoot Head].'

Another strange incident had happened several years previous to this at Cheesefoot Head. It was a dark, clear night in 1980, when two police constables were returning home from Winchester via Old Winchester Hill. It was between 1 a.m. and 2 a.m. and there were very few cars around. As the constables were driving along, they suddenly observed something coming up behind them. One constable related how he and his colleague, who was driving, saw this 'thing' coming. The best way he could describe it was that it was lit up like 'an illuminated horse' and appeared to be chasing the car. 'The thing's after us … it's going to get us. STOP, STOP THE CAR AND LET IT PASS.'

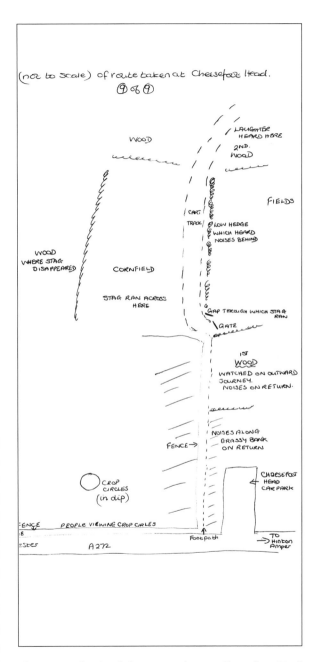

Figure 57: Sketch of the route taken at Cheesefoot Head

They were very, very frightened and wanted 'it' to overtake them, thus hopefully allowing it to go on its way. As it approached them, they stopped to let it pass. They wound down their windows to observe it more closely and it was then that it became apparent that it was no horse, despite having four legs. It made no sound and seemed shrouded in a cloak of evil.

The constable held onto his mate in terror as it passed. Within seconds it had disappeared as quickly as it had come, into terrain which was impassable. It was almost as though it had never existed in the first place. Filled with horror the two constables drove away as fast as they could. Had they not seen the 'thing' together, each would have doubted their eyes and put it down to imagination.

However, policemen are trained to observe critically and logically; they are accustomed to being placed in unusual and awkward situations and know how to cope with the unexpected; so when I spoke to one of the constables, I was surprised to hear the unmistakable fear in his voice, even after a lapse of 14 years. He could give no explanation for their experience, except to say that the atmosphere as the 'thing' went past them was 'dreadful' and they couldn't leave the area quickly enough.

Chapter Six

Effects on Animals

Whereas a number of the effects and experiences related so far might be labelled by some as the result of suggestion, expectation or wishful thinking, reports relating to the strange behaviour of animals are far more difficult to dismiss. Animals react instinctively; they cannot be party to deception. They are not connivers or colluders, nor can they be accused of having any ulterior motives or preconceived expectations. They do however often react in response to the feelings of their owners.

EFFECTS ON BEHAVIOUR

Dogs are especially agitated by crop formations. There are increasing numbers of reports, almost too many to list, of dogs reacting in an unusual fashion prior to a formation being discovered or on the night a formation appears in the vicinity. However, birds, cats and horses have all been reported to behave strangely too when around crop formations.

The Agitated Sheepdog

Two unusual formations – one resembling a sceptre and the other a frying pan containing two fried eggs – appeared one night at Ogbourne Maizey, in Wiltshire in July 1991.

The farm's sheepdog, who normally slept quietly in the kitchen, became so agitated during the night that when his owners came down the next morning they found wood splinters strewn round the kitchen floor by the door. In his endeavour to get out, the dog had almost managed to scrape a hole through the thick wooden door!

The farmer and his wife had been working very late in the fields the previous evening and that night they had fallen into a sound sleep, so they were not aware of their dog's agitated state. They also kept

Figure 58: The 'Frying Pan', Ogbourne Maizey, Wiltshire, July 1991. Wheat

some horses at livery and at 7 a.m., when the farmer's wife went round the stable yard during the horses' normal sleepy period, she found them wide awake and alert – though not agitated. 'They were clearly longing to tell me something,' she says. What had they seen or heard during the night that had left them so alert, and which had disturbed the dog to such an extent? Were they affected by subtle changes in the geomagnetic field?

Ogbourne Maizey is one of three villages rich in folklore and legend, that nestle in the valley of the river Og, Ogbourne Maizey to the south, Ogbourne St Andrew to the West and the largest of the three, Ogbourne St George to the North. They are situated along the Marlborough to Swindon road.

Rockley House and Temple Farm at Ogbourne Maizey mark the site of one of the ancient quarters of the Knights Templars. Nearby rises Hackpen Hill with its White Horse and which is situated just a few yards from the 1991 formation that appeared in the field across the road from the hill. There are also many reports of Faery happenings, including one recorded by noted historian John Aubrey which tells of a shepherd who was taken under the hill; the hill at certain phases of the moon being raised up on pillars. Music was heard and revelry was seen by the shepherd before he returned. It seems he was never quite the same after his visit beneath the hill.

This is yet another example of crop circles forming in close proximity to hill carvings, ancient monuments, tumulii and faery places.

Dance, dance, dance little croppie,
And o'er your shoulder cast a watchful glance,
For there will you glimpse the Faery folk,
Sitting beneath the ageless hill,
They know the secret thought you think,
They know the secret song you sing,
They will dance with you to the gilded circle,
Painted gold by the Full Moon Maid.
And there you will ride on the crested horse
To the place where the circles and shapes cascade,
At the edge of the earth and beyond.
At the edge of the earth and beyond.

© Lucy Pringle, 1993

Other Dogged Reports

A woman had a terrifying experience in the Hopi Symbol pictogram, the last formation to appear at The Gallops, Cheesefoot Head in early August 1990.

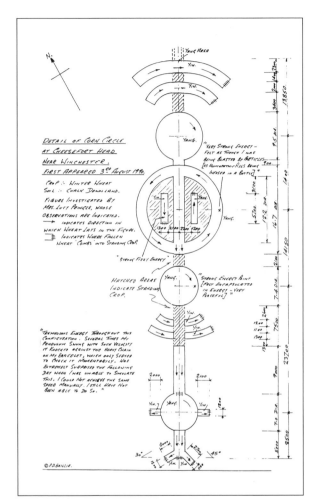

Figure 59: The Hopi symbol, The Gallops, Cheesefoot Head, Hampshire, 3 August 1990. Wheat. © Peter Baillie

She had been standing at the outer rim of the large circle at the northern end when a Rotweiller came bounding into the formation – its hapless owner calling frantically at it to stop. Quite out of control, the animal came rushing towards the petrified woman. Unable to move with fear, she remained frozen to the

ground; indeed, had she been able to move where on earth could she have gone? There was nowhere!

As the dog reached the centre of her circle, it dropped to the ground, lay over on its side and within seconds was fast asleep! What was the strange energy or force had stopped the dog dead in its tracks?

Another report concerns a woman who, during early June 1995, visited the beautiful Clutch Plate formation at Telegraph Hill, again near Cheesefoot Head. She was sitting quietly when she heard a crackling noise in the crop that seemed to get louder as it approached her. A couple joined her and the noise stopped abruptly. Her husband returned with their two Labradors who, the moment they entered the formation, attacked each other and then the unknown couple. The dogs seemed very frightened and kept pressing themselves against their owners, as if in need of comfort and reassurance. They were taken out of the formation and immediately returned to their normal, playful selves.

We know that, at certain electromagnetic frequencies, animals tested in laboratory conditions have attacked the nearest living creature. It therefore seems likely that whatever frequencies were present at the formation were responsible for the unusual behaviour of the dogs in these instances.

Also in 1995, a dog and its owner visited the Silbury Hill Flower.

'My dog appeared to be affected by the atmosphere and acted strangely. He was bouncing around very excitedly and kept jumping up at me all the while. When I sat down he laid his head and paws across me – he has never done this before. Then he sat back-to-back with me. He did not seem to want to leave me to explore by himself.'

Effects on Birds

Birds can be affected by crop formations just as much as dogs and other mammals. In this case a flock of Canada geese were feeding approximately a kilometre from the Watmough formation, near Lethbridge, in Canada.

On several occasions various-sized groups would leave the flock and head off for a destination in line with the crop circle formation. Every single time a group approached the formation, they were observed to detour round the circle, veering off to one side or the other, and then continue on their original course. Sometimes a group would split up, some geese flying to one side, some to the other, only to regroup after effectively clearing the formation. Not once did any of the geese fly directly over the configuration. At least 100 birds took part in this ritual, flying at a height of between 30 and 35 feet (9–10.5m). They seemed to be sensing (and avoiding) some sort of energy which was rising vertically from the circle. Chad Deetken observed them:

'In order not to influence the geese in any way, I crouched down low and remained in that position long before any of them came close to the formation. After the birds had passed the site, they flew over people and moving vehicles with no indication of fear or unusual caution.'

Horse Sense

A beautiful Daisy Chain formation in barley was dis-covered at Cheriton, near Cheesefoot Head, Hampshire on 6 July 1997 (*see Figure 16, page 16*). The surrounding 29 circles around the flattened centre each contained a tuft of standing crop; diagonally across the centre of the formation were two 'magi-mix' blades consisting of minute and perfect circles.

An American researcher was the first to discover and visit this formation. She had neglected to get the farmer's permission and, as she was standing in the circle, the farmer's wife came riding down the tramline towards her. As the woman got nearer, she rode towards the researcher in an aggressive manner, but the moment her horse reached the edge of the circle it stopped and, despite several cracks of the whip, refused to budge, becoming quite agitated. This clearly added to the rider's annoyance, and she shouted, 'I do not believe in these *** circles!'

'Maybe you don't, but your horse certainly does!' replied the researcher.

Animals, particularly horses, are hypersensitive to

Figure 60a: Solar/Lunar eternity symbol, Liddington Castle, near Swindon, Wiltshire, 29 July 1996. Wheat

Figure 60b: Close up of the eternity symbol, showing the crop layering 'wave'

electro-magnetic fields and can detect these energies in a way no human can.

Cats are other animals that are also extremely sensitive to energies and 'vibes', and are particularly drawn to high energies, especially high negative energies.

Luke, a blue Burmese, often went for jaunts with his owner in the countryside. However, in 1997 towards the end of summer, he visited his first crop formation – the Solar/Lunar Eternity Symbol below Liddington Castle, near Swindon.

Luke was unusually ill at ease and disturbed by the experience; his owner, in contrast, was contented and relaxed.

Remote Effects on Animals

Just as humans seem to be affected at remote distances from the crop formations so, it seems, are animals.

My own excellent and enormous grey cat, Hero, seemed to be receiving a regular 'fix' from barley samples collected from the Beckhampton spiral formation. During the summer of 1995 I collected several samples from formations I had visited. Amongst them were samples taken from the Avebury Trusloe Spiral, in which many people, myself included, suffered severe adverse reactions.

One day I noticed Hero sitting over the barley samples, sucking them avidly. I had to remove him

Figure 61: Spiral at Beckhampton, Wiltshire, 29 May 1995. Barley

physically from the room. Each time I opened the dining-room door he made a bee-line for the samples, resuming his sucking. I then noticed that he regularly started to take up guard outside the door, as though he had some compulsion to enter.

During this same time he became very vicious, savaging me on several occasions. This was alarming, quite contrary to his normal behaviour and totally out of character. However, by March 1996 I suddenly realized that Hero was back to his normal self and that when I opened the dining-room door, he no longer hurtled in as though the hounds of hell were after him. The samples of barley were still there, albeit slightly the worse for wear, but he ignored them. Whatever the effects had been, they had obviously worn off, or Hero had become immune to them.

PHYSICAL EFFECTS OF FORMATIONS

There are reports from a few places, including North America, on the destructive force of the energies generated during the creation of the crop circles.

The Flattened Porcupines

On the night of 21 August 1992, four miles (6.4 km) south of the village of Milestone, southern Saskatchewan, Canadian farmer Joe Rennick discovered an irregular rectangular formation, about 22 feet by 63 feet (6.7 m x 19 m), in his wheat field.

'It looked as though a round object had come down and skipped several times like a flat stone on water. Never having seen a crop formation before, I thought that it had been caused by wind damage but, on closer observation, I noted a roughly laid counter-clockwise swirl. Walking into the centre I noticed something else – a very flat and very dead porcupine.'

Chad Deetken, the Canadian researcher, examined the corpse carefully and could find no signs of any injury. The porcupine gave every indication of having been steamrollered. Clearly some considerable weight had been applied (see Figure 62). Despite the farmer not finding the formation for approximately seven days, the animal did not smell and there were no visible signs of decomposition.

An adult porcupine is not a small animal. It can weigh around 20lbs (2.26kg) (and possibly up to 25lbs – 2.8kg), and is around 12 inches (30cm) in height. Chad recalls that this one 'had been flattened to a thickness of three inches (7cms), its legs spread out underneath it in the form of an X'.

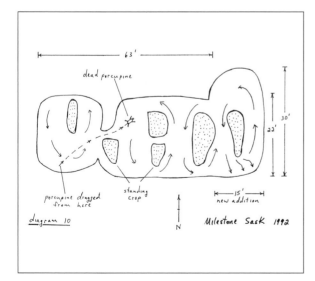

Figure 62: Diagram © Chad Deetken

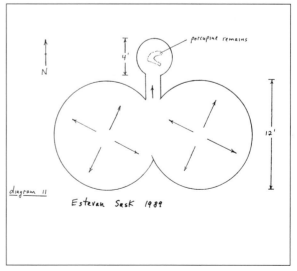

Figure 63: Diagram © Chad Deetken

It also appeared (from the scrape marks and a row of standing broken quills) to have been dragged in to the centre of the formation from the perimeter. The flow of the flattened quills on its body went in the same direction as the lay of the fallen crop.

Another strange anomaly of the formation was the dryness, 'like cement', of the soil within the circle in comparison to the 'sticky' quality of the soil outside. Chad reported that:

'The imprints of the fallen stalks were clearly visible on the ground as though the stalks had been forcefully slammed down. Also the plants in the field were still green and supple, but in the formation they were extremely dry and brittle, and the seeds were dried like prunes.'

This report fits in with the 'vaporization' theory mentioned by several researchers in their findings. The energy, which appears to have sucked the poor creature to its doom, seems to have eluded quantum physicists; so far we do not have instruments sensitive enough to detect or record it.

Animals seem able to tune into seismic and atmospheric vibrations and are thus given prior notice of approaching danger long before we are, often some considerable time before the event actually occurs. How then can we explain why the porcupine got caught up in the energy or force? The answer would seem to be that porcupines, like hedgehogs, rely on their pointed quills to protect them and when danger approaches they freeze until the way is clear once more.

Three years earlier in late July 1989, four miles (6.4 km) north of Estevan, Saskatchewan, and about 100 miles (168km) south-east of Milestone, farmer Don Hagel found two 12-foot (3.6m) touching circles in one of his wheat fields (Figure 63). The lay was radial in both cases. A narrow path ending in a small circle abutted from the point at which the circles met. It was in this small connected circle that he, too, found a dead porcupine.

He estimated by the contrast in growth between the fallen crop in the circle and the standing crop outside, that the animal had been dead for about two to three weeks. Both he and his wife particularly noticed that the only bits left were the quills and bones – no flesh or skin anywhere – and that part of the jaw and tail-bone appeared to be missing.

The strangest part of all this, however, was the blackness of the remains – like soot. Neither the farmer nor his wife were able to rub this off. The ground under the animal was also darkened. Despite having lived on the land all their lives, the couple swore that they had never seen anything like it before and that 'no predator nor ants or anything else could account for the condition of the remains'.

It is reminiscent of cases of spontaneous combustion in humans – which has been postulated to be caused by a short circuit of electro-chemical energy. This phenomenon has been known to exist for some time; Charles Dickens talks about Krook, the rag-and-bone man, in *Bleak House*, who met an untimely death by spontaneous combustion (thought to have been caused by an abnormal consumption of alcohol), leaving behind nothing of himself except 'something on the floor' at which the cat snarled, and his cap and jacket hanging on a chair. 'There is a smouldering suffocating vapour in the room, and a dark greasy coating on the walls and ceiling.'

In the Saskatchewan case the farmer called in the police, who originally thought that some sort of Satanic worship might have been involved. The police instructed the laboratory where tissue samples were being analysed to look for burning. The results showed no evidence that any burning had taken place.

The Exploded Birds

The only instance on this side of the Atlantic of animals being damaged by the circle-making force came in the summer of 1993. It occurred in the first of five formations to appear in a near straight line, stretching over a distance of five miles from Wanborough in Surrey to the outskirts of Guildford, in a matter of less than two weeks.

Fellow researcher, Christopher Weeks, telephoned me one evening. 'Come as soon as you can. Something has exploded in a crop formation.' It was too dark to set out that evening so I arranged to meet Christopher the following day. We entered the ringed formation and there were the remains just as he had described – numerous small feathers strewn over a radius of 13 to 14 feet (4–4.2m) from the centre of the circle. From the way the blood and feathers were present in every layer of the crop, right down to the ground, it was apparent that the birds had been caught up in the actual creation of the formation, blown apart and disintegrated by the force. Mixed in with the blood and feathers were minute bits of flesh, but there were no bones, nor any distinguishable or recognizable parts.

We sent a sample to be blind-tested in a laboratory and the message came back that it looked as though 'a bird had exploded'. It has been suggested that the

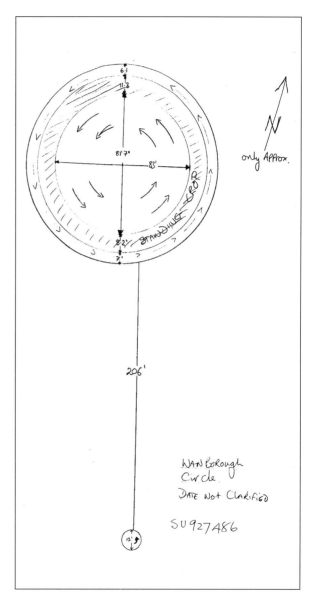

Figure 64: Diagram of the ringed circle and satellite at Wanborough, near Guildford, Surrey, 27 July 1993. Wheat. © Christopher Weeks

birds could have been dead already. I like this idea and indeed consider it likely for there are many foxes in the area, as well as people shooting pigeons. Indeed, a fox had already killed a pigeon and left its feathers in a tidy pile in the outer ring of the formation, although this was quite distinct from the widespread 'mess' within the circle.

What sort of force can explode a bird? Some form of microwave activity must be present and this could be responsible, and indeed the charring effect evidenced by the porcupine in the report above would go some way to confirming this.

This idea of electromagnetic/microwave energy can also help explain the strange effects crop circles have on mechanical equipment – the subject of the next chapter.

Right Dumb-bell and boxes, Crawely Down, Hampshire, July 1990. Wheat. © Terence Meaden

Below The Silbury Hill area. Drawing by William Stukeley.
© Wiltshire Archaeological and Natural History Society, Devizes

Prospect of the Temple on Overton Hill. 8 July 1723.

TAB. XX
P. 40

Ranibuy   w. road   Ro. Camp   Silbury   Windmill bill   Abury

Stukeley d.

The Hakpen, or head of the Snake, in ruins.

North/South formation. Avebury Trusloe, Wiltshire. 14 June 1991. Length 179 ft (54m). Barley

The narrow two-inch (5cms) band of fallen crop at Avebury Trusloe, 9 June 1991. Barley

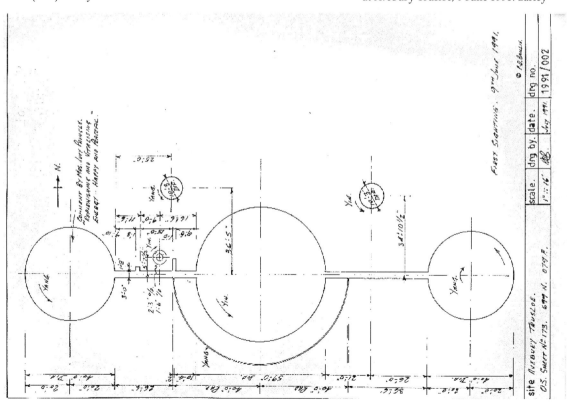

Diagram of Avebury Trusloe west/east formation, 9 June 1991. Barley. © Peter Baillie

Half Ringed dumb-bell. Froxfield, Wiltshire, 19 August 1991. *c.*150 ft (45m) long. Wheat.
© Andrew King

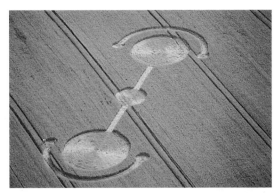

'Key Pictogram'. East Kennett, Wiltshire, 27 July 1991. Length 305 ft (92m). Wheat. © Terence Meaden

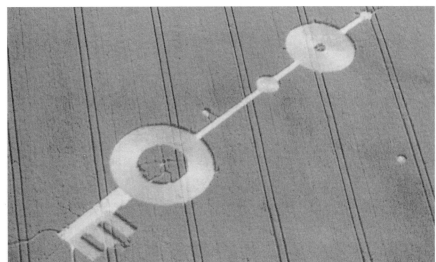

'Key Pictogram'. Preschute Down, Wiltshire, July 1991. Length 250 ft (76m). Wheat.
© Terence Meaden

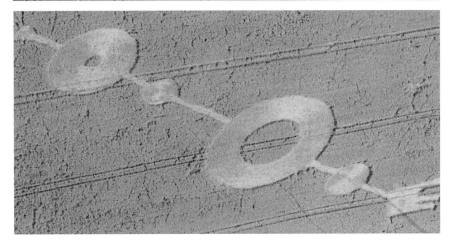

Triangular Triplet. Olivers Castle, near Devizes, Wiltshire, 24 July 1992. Wheat. Circle diameters 30 ft (9m), adjoining paths 30 ft (9m) long.
© Jürgen Kronig

Triangular Triplet. Olivers Castle, near Devizes, Wiltshire, 24 July 1992. Wheat

Milk Hill hieroglyph, Wiltshire, early August 1991. *c.*240 ft (73m) long. Wheat. © Andrew King

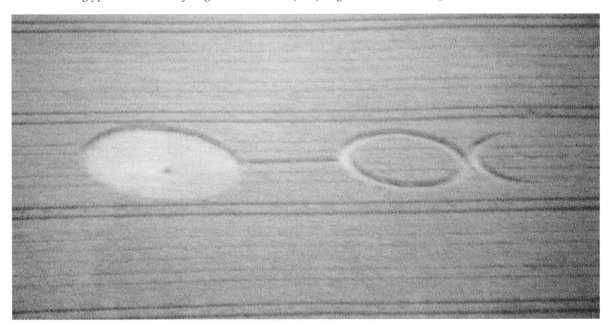

'Mercury', West Stowell, Wiltshire, 2 August 1992. 131 ft (40m) long. Wheat. © Grant Wakefield

Right Circle with crescent. Draycott Farm, Wiltshire. 9 August 1992. Diameter 65 ft (20m). Wheat. © Grant Wakefield

Below 'Mercury', West Stowell, Wiltshire, 9 August 1992. Wheat. © Grant Wakefield

Above Small pictogram. Goodworth
Clatford, near Andover, Hampshire,
29 June 1993. Wheat. Showing
interweaving

Right Small pictogram. Goodworth
Clatford, near Andover, Hampshire,
29 June 1993. Diameter 60 ft (18m).
Wheat

Below Flexford, near Guildford,
Surrey, 6 August 1993. Wheat

Right Infinity symbol, West Overton, Wiltshire, 28 July 1994. Diameter. *c*.130 ft (39m). Wheat

Below 'Galaxy', Froxfield, Wiltshire, 4 August 1994. Diameter 360 ft (109m). Wheat

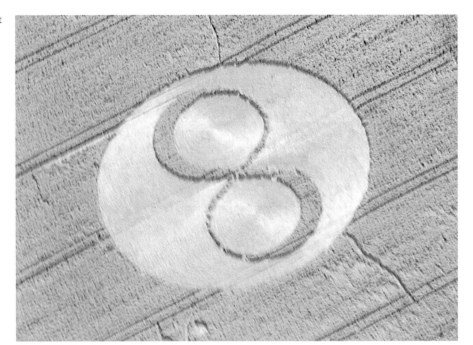

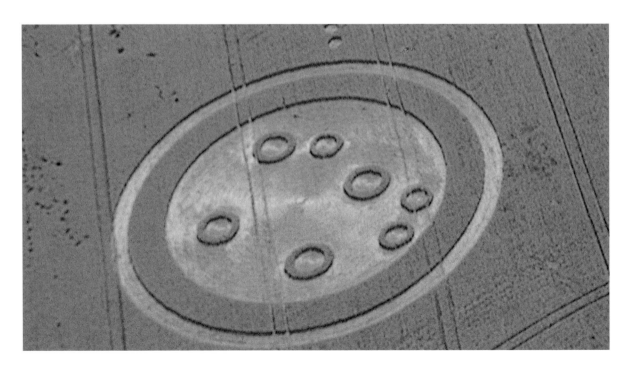

Right 'Caduceus', Litchfield, Hampshire, 6 July 1995. *c.*220 ft (66m) diameter. Wheat

Below Roundway Hill, Devizes, Wiltshire, 23 July 1995. Diameter 210 ft (64m). Wheat

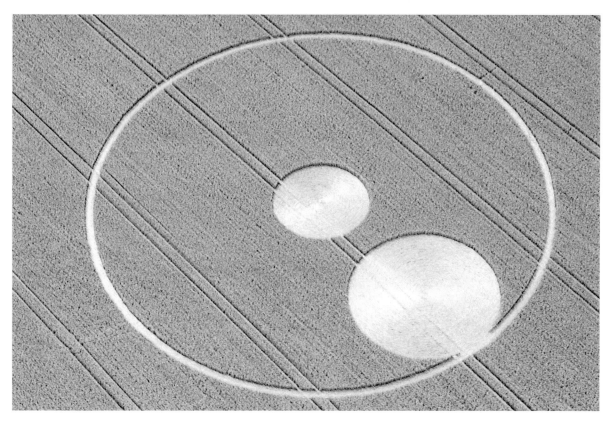

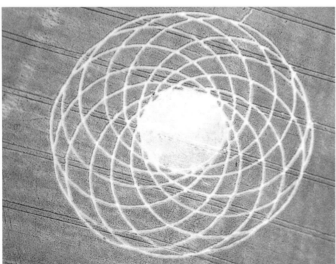

Above 'Pentacle', Bishops
Canning, Wiltshire, 13 July 1997.
c.180 ft (55m) diameter. Wheat

Left 'Torus Knot', Alton Priors,
Wiltshire, 11 July 1997. 12 rings,
diameter in excess of 500 ft
(152m). Wheat

West Tisted, Hampshire, showing the layering of the crop. 26 July 1996. Wheat

West Tisted, Hampshire, one of the outer rings showing man-made interference. 26 July 1996. Wheat

Celtic Cross, Morestead, Hampshire, 21 July 1997. 152 ½ft (46m) diameter. Wheat

Above 'Vesica Pisces' in reverse. Cutforth, Wiltshire, 21 June 1998. Overall length *c*.180 ft (55m). Wheat

'Vesica Pisces'. Clatford, Wiltshire, 22 June 1998. Overall length *c*.120 ft (36m). Barley

'Dreamcatcher', Cley Hill, near Warminster, Wiltshire, 14 July 1997. 220 ft (66m) diameter. Wheat

Centre of the 'Whale', The Firs, near Beckhampton, Wiltshire, 1 August 1991. Wheat

Centre of a section of the 'Charm Bracelet', Silbury Hill. 16 August 1992. Wheat

'Square', Silbury, Wiltshire, 23 July 1998. Overall length *c*.250 ft (76m). Wheat

Pilot dies as aircraft plunges into field

WITNESSES watched horror as a light aircraft crashed and burst into flames in a field on the outskirts of Guildford early on Sunday morning, killing the lone pilot.

The twin-engined Piper 31, an air taxi, skimmed houses in Warren Road and

by Ann Dent

Mr Nicklin, a Guildford optician, is a pilot and has shared ownership of a Piper single engine Saratoga.

The twin-engine Piper shot out of the clouds at about 200 mph. Both engines were going. It ploughed straight down into the earth

headed to the ground.

Supt Stan Harland, of Guildford police, who was one of the first of the emergency services on the scene, said the wreckage was confined to a small area. There had been several witnesses and a report that the plane was on fire before it hit the ground.

The first police officer to arrive, PC Phil Moss said it

Figure 71: Headline in the Surrey Advertiser newspaper on 20 August 1993. © Surrey Advertiser

that Roger Nicklin and his companion were cycling, as was their custom, along the track on the north side of the ridge that runs from Pewley Down to Longdown.

Mr Nicklin, an optician and pilot from Guildford, describes what happened next.

'We set off just after 7 o'clock, it was a cold morning and I became aware of an aircraft just above the clouds, a two engine aircraft just above the clouds to my left; soon after that the aircraft appeared in a steep dive as it emerged from the cloud, the right wing slightly low and it headed straight into the ground. There was a very large explosion. I immediately turned round and came home to 'phone for the police and emergency services and instructed my friend to continue to the site of the crash, to see if he could assist the pilot. I followed along about five minutes later. All that was left of the aircraft was a mangled lump of wreckage and there was nothing left of the pilot apart from a few unrecognizable lumps of meat.'

It seemed that the impact had thrown the pilot forward and any remains were found scattered in small, unrecognizable pieces just over a small wire fence.

'The base of the cloud was about 1,000 ft [303m], so the pilot was flying above that level. It was hard to tell where he was in between layers of cloud when he started his dive, but when he appeared through the cloud he was already in a more-or-less vertical dive.'

Roger Nicklin feels he must have already been out of control whilst in cloud and it would seem likely that he was already unconscious when he started his dive in excess of 1,000 feet (303m). According to Roger Nicklin both engines were working and he made no attempt to close the throttles or pull the aircraft out of the dive.

'Even if he had been out of control, having lost control of one of the control services, he would still have closed the throttles to reduce the speed and tried to turn the aircraft. He made no effort to do any of these things.'

Roger Nicklin states that it was a clear morning underneath the cloud and, being a pilot himself, he is accustomed to observing and listening to aircraft, and until the aircraft appeared in a dive he was unaware that anything was amiss. He estimates that the pilot was travelling at about 200 mph (322kph) and that he impacted the ground at an angle far greater than the 30 degrees reported, 'unless he had tried at the last minute to pull out'.

The pilot was on his way from Romford to Southampton and he had been talking to the VOR station at Wisley Airfield, (a radio station) and had just said goodbye to London control which is on the edge of the zone at Ockham. He would have been travelling to Southampton passing probably to the north of Guildford. When Roger saw him he was 'coming from a rather strange direction, from the west of Guildford and assuming that he was travelling from east to west, that was unusual'.

Roger feels that it was unlikely that he would have committed suicide as he had no idea where he was going. When he came out of the cloud he was already in a dive and apparently his radio messages had sounded normal, i.e., London was not alerted that there might be a problem. Roger imagined he must have been unconscious. His health would have been very good as he was a commercial pilot and subject to stringent and regular class one medical tests.

One of the hypotheses had been that a very large bird like a Canada goose, which have been known to fly above clouds, might have gone through the windscreen and incapacitated him, but with plastic raked windscreens it seems unlikely and there was no evidence of any feathers. Apparently there have also been reports of crashes due to propellers falling off that model of aircraft, but not in this case as both propellers were there and both engines were working. It seems that the pilot was incapacitated in some way for even had he been disorientated and lost control, he would have had ample time to make amends and pull the aircraft up once he emerged from the cloud. It is a horrifying thought that he dived for 1,000 feet (303m).

There were two hot air balloons also coming from the west, but Roger makes no connection between

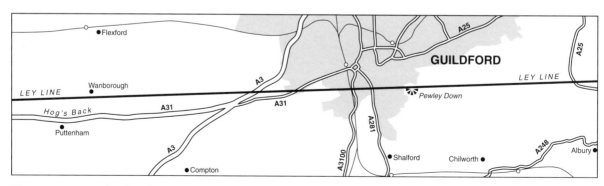

Figure 72: OS Map showing the energy line running east and west of Guildford. Line plotted by Christopher Weeks

the two events, as they were some distance apart.

We walked along Pewley Down to the site of the crash. The ground had been levelled off and apart from the remains of ribbons which had been attached to the many bouquets left by wellwishers, there was nothing to be seen. The crater had been filled in.

This air crash is of such a puzzling nature and so many people have remarked on the uncanny similarities to the occurrences which befall aircraft in the Bermuda Triangle area, that it seems only proper to discuss it in some detail. The report (reproduced at the end of this chapter) from the Air Accident Investigation Association at Farnborough, tells us what happened in greater detail.

In early February 1994, the coroner returned an open verdict, having failed to establish any conclusive evidence into the crash or the death of the pilot. The investigation had taken longer than normal due to the extensive damage to the plane, thereby hampering normal engineering analysis and reconstruction.

Roland Shimmons, Department of Transport inspector of Air Accident Investigations at Farnborough said the pilot was qualified to fly on instruments if visibility was a problem. The flight as we can see from the report had been tracked by radar from Heathrow and radio messages were recorded until a minute before the accident. This last message gave no indication that anything was amiss. Dr Henry Drysdale, RAF Institute of Pathology consultant said the body was so mutilated he could neither confirm or deny any sudden trauma or natural death prior to the crash.

George Galanopoulos, Chief Pilot for the aircraft firm who had trained the deceased pilot on the Piper Navajo, said he found him an above average and meticulously conscientious pilot who spent a lot of time preparing for a flight and working out his routes. He was experienced in European flights, and was accustomed to landing his plane in both busy commercial airports and isolated landing strips. Being a commercial pilot he would have been required to take regular and intensive medical tests. George Galanopoulos said, 'he seemed fit and well and two weeks before the accident he was very happy. His life was in order. He was happy his divorce was going through and his career was advancing as he was flying a larger aircraft'.

An interesting postscript to this gruesome story is that an energy line rising at Newlands Corner, east of Guildford, passes not only directly through the crash site at Pewley Down but continues through the crop formation sites at Flexford Farm and Wanborough. Extending the line west it passes directly through Farnham, Andover, and the sacred Woodhenge site, before finally piercing Glastonbury Cathedral; extending it eastward it passes directly through Dorking, Reigate and Maidstone, before coming to rest at Canterbury, revealing that the line lies along the ancient Pilgrim's Way.

Note

The effect that crop circles obviously have on mechanical and electronic equipment, and especially on batteries, clearly raises possible health problems for people who have cardiac pacemakers and other such equipment fitted. I would strongly advise these people to exercise extreme caution when entering crop formations.

Appendix – Air Accident Report on Pewley Down Aircrash

Aircraft Type and Registration: Piper PA-31 Navajo, G-SEAS.

No. and Type of Engines: 2 Lycoming TIO-540-A2C piston engines.

Year of Manufacture: 1979.

Date and Time (UTC): 15 August 1993 at 0705hrs.

Location: Pewley Down, near Guildford, Surrey.

Type of Flight: Public Transport (positioning).

Persons on Board: Crew - 1. Passengers - None.

Injuries: Crew - Fatal. Passengers - N/A.

Nature of Damage: Aircraft destroyed.

Commander's Licence: Commercial Pilot's Licence with Instrument Rating.

Commander's Age: 33 years.

Commander's Flight Experience: 1,493 hours (of which 440 were multi-engined and 15 were on type). Last 90 days - 162 hours. Last 28 days - 50 hours.

Information source: AAIB Field Investigation.

'The pilot was rostered to fly from his home base at Stapleford to Southampton on a positioning flight. He was due to pick up passengers at Southampton and fly to Cambridge where more were to be collected; from Cambridge he would fly to Berlin. For the return he would fly back to Cambridge, unload some passengers and be relieved by another pilot. The day prior to the accident the pilot had a two hour flight, and then spent four hours planning the Berlin flight with the assistance of his Chief Pilot. Following the planning the two pilots made a comprehensive check of G-SEAS and refuelled to full tanks.

'On the 15 August the pilot arrived at the airfield at 0605 hrs and opened the flight offices. Shortly afterwards an assistant arrived and saw the pilot of G-SEAS doing some pre-flight paperwork. The assistant then opened the clubhouse and had a short conversation with the pilot who had come in to prepare for his prospective passengers; the pilot appeared to be in normal spirits. Subsequently, the assistant saw the pilot doing external checks on G-SEAS, heard the aircraft being taxied away at approximately 0635 hrs, and then heard it take off at approximately 0645hrs. The assistant stated that, at the time, the weather at Stapleford was warm with a light haze and that he could not see any cloud.'

The report then reconstructs the flight using air-to-ground radio recordings from London and Farnborough ATC, and secondary radar recordings from Heathrow, Pease Pottage and Deben. The radio recordings show that the pilot of G-SEAS was using callsign STL 819. At 0658 hrs, eight minutes before the fatal crash, Heathrow called STL 819 to inform him that there was another aircraft, Ascot 7963, holding over Ockham at 1,500 feet (455m) amsl (above mean sea level). When Heathrow informed the holding aircraft of the approach of STL 819, the Ascot pilot stated that he was climbing to 2,400 feet (727m) amsl. Shortly afterwards, the captain of Ascot 7963 saw an aircraft passing below him in a normal attitude tracking towards Ockham. STL 819 was given clearance to leave Heathrow for Farnborough, having been advised that Farnborough might not be open.

At 0704 hrs STL 819 called on Farnborough but

had no reply as indeed the airfield was not yet open. This was the last radio call recorded from STL 819.

'The radar recordings confirmed the track of STL 819 to Ockham and from there the aircraft made a gentle left turn onto a track of approximately 185°T; all three radars confirmed the aircraft speed as approximately 160kt [knots] and at a level altitude of 1,500 feet [455m] amsl until a few seconds before 0705 hrs. At that point the aircraft started a high rate of descent with increasing speed but maintaining a fairly constant southerly track. Radar contact was lost 2.6 seconds after 0705 hrs.

'An aftercast obtained from the Meteorological Office at Bracknell indicated the following weather conditions at the time of the accident; 5,000 metres visibility, no mist, no fog or rain, scattered stratus base 1,200 feet [364m] amsl and broken stratocumulus base 5,000 feet [1,515m] amsl. This accords with the estimate from the Ascot pilot.'

Engineering investigation

The report goes on to describe the location of the crash as being a field of pasture just north of the crest of Pewley Down.

'The direction of travel at impact had been 191°M which accords closely with the aircraft's final track seen on radar. Wreckage was spread over a distance of 160 feet [48m] from the impact with a few individual items being thrown somewhat further. The aircraft had been fragmented by the impact and there had been an intense fire which had melted or consumed much of the aluminium structure. The aircraft had hit the ground at high speed and in a steep dive.

'Measurements obtained from the ground suggested a dive angle of 30° to 35° and evidence later obtained from the aircraft's indicting system indicated that, at impact, the aircraft's speed had been substantially in excess of its certified maximum speed of 236kt. The initial impact had left an impression on the ground which corresponded with the frontal aspect of the aircraft. There was an imprint of the leading edge of the wing complete from one wingtip to the other and the engines had come to rest, embedded in the ground, just forward of their impact positions. The impact evidence showed that the aircraft had been upright, banked slightly to the right and yawed significantly to the left when it hit the ground. The impact evidence, either from the ground marks or the airframe wreckage, showed no indication of the aircraft being pitched up relative to its flightpath, ie, no evidence of any attempted recovery from the dive.

'From the extensive area of burnt and withered grass which became apparent over the following twenty four hours, it was clear that fuel had been splashed over a very wide area, indicating that there had been a large amount of fuel in the tanks in both wings.'

The wreckage was taken to Farnborough where it was examined in detail and all relevant tests performed.

'The aircraft and its internal components had been crushed, fragmented and burned and the recovered material included a large amount of ash.

'The aircraft had been complete at impact in terms of its essential structure and flying surfaces. Flaps and landing gear had been retracted. Evidence was found that the main cabin door and the forward baggage door were in place and latched. No evidence was found of a large bird impact on the aircraft's wing leading edges or tail. Fragments of the pilot's windscreen were collected, examined for fluoresce. No evidence was found of a bird impact but the amount of material which was collected probably amounted to less than half of the windscreen. Evidence was found that the locking pins for the pilot's seat had been engaged in the seat rails at impact.

'Not all the control system components recovered from the wreckage could be individually identified but all the failures in such components were in overload and were thus consistent with being a result of the crash. No failure or defect in the controls could be identified as being pre-existing. The propellers had both sustained rotational damage at impact. This damage was almost identical between the two propellers and it would appear, therefore, that at impact there had not been a problem of asymmetric power.'

Chapter Eight

Luminosities, UFOs and Other Realities

Luminosities, or balls of bright, moving light rather like ball lightning, have often been associated with crop formations, as we shall see. These luminosities can have a dramatic effect on the brain, due to the electromagnetic fields they generate.

Michael Persinger, a neuro-scientist at Laurentian University of Sudbury, Ontario, has investigated the effects of magnetic stimulation on the brain. Research has shown that by stimulating two areas of the brain magnetically (the amygdala and hippocampus – the areas relating to memory and meaning), a torrent of images of past memories were released, which assumed a tremendous sense of reality and importance to the patient. Further research (reported in *New Scientist*, 19 November 1994) revealed that stimulation of other areas of the brain, in particular the temporal lobes, resulted in all manner of mystical experiences, out-of-body sensations and other seemingly paranormal phenomena. Persinger also found

that abduction and UFO reports were considerably more frequent during the weeks before earthquakes, when natural magnetic effects are increased.

Magnetic fields, however, are not always beneficial. According to Persinger, 'Exposure to intense magnetic fields has been associated with an increase in cancers of the blood, brain and sexual organs and a rise in depression, suicide and alcohol abuse.'

LUMINOSITIES AND CROP CIRCLES

Is there a link between crop circles and luminosities? It would appear that the large majority of both genuine and hoaxed formations can be found on natural energy lines. That energy lines affect us more than we realize, due to their electro-magnetic emissions, is still not generally recognized.

There are ever-increasing reports of lights being

seen at the time of crop circle formations (such as when the Avebury Double Helix appeared in 1996, *see page 89*). As yet, however, we have no hard evidence of a light and a circle being directly connected – only eyewitness accounts.

A Wiltshire couple were asleep in bed on the night of 31 May 1993 when they were woken by an 'enormously' bright light shining through their window. They both got up to investigate and observed the light shining over Silbury Hill. The following morning a single-ringed formation with a radial lay to the

Figure 73: Anomalies caught on camera by David Kingston. © David Kingston

crop was discovered in a field directly opposite Silbury Hill.

After Rachael Martineau and her husband had visited the large pictogram that graced East Field, Alton Barnes, in 1991 she felt compelled to walk to the tip of the formation, where it became very narrow.

'Here I felt a lot of pressure both on top and underneath me, and I got a sudden very, very bad headache and felt sick. As I was walking out of the tip and into the first big circle I noticed a whitish light coming across the field. It slowly hovered over the crop round the field and came within 15 feet [4.5m] of where I was. It was a mass of tiny, pulsing lights, shaped like a doughnut – that is, a fat outer ring with a narrow middle.

'It was about three feet [a metre] across and just one foot [0.3m] high. It didn't come up to me particularly so I was surprised that no one else seemed to notice it; rather it just passed by near me. As I watched it, I could also see red streaks like tiny lightning flashes in the sky above the crop. The shaped light was orangey/white (much more white than orange). Then it drifted off and speeded up and zoomed off over the hill.

'Later that day, in Bristol, I could see big bouncing orange balls of light (about four during the afternoon) about three feet [a metre] in diameter. They were following us, bouncing into people and being "absorbed" or dissipating into them!'

On another occasion a well-known 'cropscape' artist was engrossed in creating a pattern in a field of wheat, when he felt he was being 'watched'. He looked up and saw a brilliant light in the sky, engulfing him in its beam. It remained in a stationary position and he felt more and more uncomfortable. Who or what was monitoring his illicit activities? He completed his work hurriedly and, with the light still hanging in the sky, he left.

The photographs in Figure 73 were taken by David Kingston, who runs Crop Phenomena Investigations in Dorset. On 30 August 1994 he had a telephone call from a farmer, who had discovered three formations on his land when he was about to start harvesting his crops.

David grabbed his camera, which had a fresh roll of film in it, and rushed to the field containing the first formation. He noticed strong magnetic anomalies, as his compass swung wildly for some 15 minutes. On leaving the formation he felt as if something were approaching him, and the hairs on the back of his neck stood on end. He took three photographs facing the unknown and invisible 'presence', and he used up the remainder of the film (33 exposures) taking pictures of the other two formations.

When the film was developed only the first three photographs came out – the rest of the film was 'fogged'. He contacted the development company, who suggested that he had either been near X-ray machines or through a security check at an airport. Clearly this was not the case and, unable to find anyone who could give him an explanation, David contacted an American company, who requested that they be sent not only the photographs, but the negatives and the camera. These were duly despatched, and the report came back that the objects David had caught on film were three-dimensional and solid.

Marlborough Lights

The summer of 1992 welcomed an abundance of crop formations in the Marlborough area of Wiltshire. Naturally occurring geological energy lines abound in this ancient place, the most famous being the Michael and Mary lines stretching from Carn Les Boel in Cornwall, though the West country on a line to Hopton in Norfolk.

Paul Vigay, inventor and computer expert (*see page 92*), recounts that the Centre for Crop Circle Studies, along with its American cousins, was involved in a research project collecting crop and soil samples for investigation and analysis. Also on the agenda was research into mechanical failures and electromagnetic anomalies. Paul found himself spending a great deal of time in the Marlborough area.

Paul had been staying at Alton Barnes, a small village nestling alongside its equally small neighbour, Alton Priors. It has been suggested that 'Alton' is the Saxon word for spring, and indeed there are many springs in the area which must have made it an attractive area to the earliest farming communities.

If you approach from the east in the direction of Lockeridge Road you will find the superb defensive site of the Neolithic Causewayed enclosure of Knap Hill. Descending the hill, the natural amphitheatre of the 550-acre (223ha) East Field, the home of the first crop circle 'pictogram' in July 1990, opens out on your left. Further down the hill on your right you will see a White Horse carved into the chalk hill side of the Wansdyke, measuring 166 feet high by 160 feet long (50m by 48m).

Paul was returning home to Hampshire late one evening.

'At approximately 11.30 p.m. I left Alton Barnes, driving towards Honey Street. The weather was wet but not raining. As I reached Honey Street I could see some bends in the road ahead, shown by the light from my headlamps. As I neared them I saw an approaching bright glow from further down the road, beyond the bends. I assumed this was a car approaching from the opposite direction and slowed down in preparation.

'As I neared the bends a single, bright headlamp raced around the corner travelling at approximately 50 to 60 mph [80–100kph]. I thought it was a motorcycle, although the light seemed lower to the ground than a headlamp – perhaps 12 to 18 inches [30–45cms] above the road surface. Seeing the excessive speed at which the object was travelling, I stopped to allow it past, still assuming it was a motorcycle. As it came to within 10 to 20 yards [9–18m] in front of me, instead of swerving to go round me, the object changed direction at a tangent to the ground and flew up and over the roof of my car. As the object flew approximately 10 feet [3m] above the roof, so the car stalled. This was not my error as I had stopped and the engine was idling. The car has never stalled in this situation before.

'Although the engine stalled, presumably due to electrical failure, I did notice that my headlamps remained on during the experience and that I did not notice the brightness drop. As soon as I was aware of what had happened, approximately five to ten seconds after the object flew over the roof, I wound down the window and opened the sunroof to look behind me, but the object had totally disappeared.

'As the object flew over the car I noticed that it

seemed to be emitting light from all angles – unlike a headlamp, which shines from one side – though the light was so bright I couldn't make out the shape of the object because of the glow surrounding it.

'I drove back towards Alton Barnes to see if I could find where the object went to, but I did not see it again.'

UFOS AND CROP CIRCLES

Unidentified flying objects seem to have captured the popular imagination, although many people seem to associate UFOs with alien beings from outer space, rather than the proper, more exact meaning – flying objects which are unable (at present) to be identified. This is not to say that there isn't other life in the universe apart from on Earth. As Dr James Fletcher of NASA says, 'Scientists are convinced that there are other planets with intelligent life on them.' Professor Paul Santorini, an eminent Greek scientist, goes a step further, stating:

It cannot be excluded that on other planets today there are living organisms hundreds of millions of years in advance of life on Earth, and scientific principles entirely undreamed of by Man, who is not even the last word on his own planet, let alone the last word in the universe.

UFO reports, which need to be carefully sifted and analysed, continue to pour in from people who have visited crop fields.

Is there more UFO activity than previously?

I think maybe the answer lies in an awakened interest in paranormal events, including UFOs. Certain areas are credited with unusual UFO activity, but is this simply due to the fact that there are more people watching that area? Maybe if other areas were watched with the same vigilance, the number of sightings would also increase.

Crop Formations and UFOs

On the night of 26/27 July 1992 there was a dramatic UFO sighting at Woodborough Hill, Wiltshire, associated with a crop circle appearing.

Chris Mansell became fascinated by crop formations in 1989 as an annexe to his interest in prehistoric cave and rock carvings, and related symbolism. Chris, a former lecturer at Newcastle University, Sunderland Polytechnic and Falmouth College of Art, is a regular visitor to Alton Barnes during the summer months and knows the countryside like the back of his hand.

In 1992 Chris became involved by accident in the UFO research being carried out by Dr Steven Greer in the area around Alton Barnes. Dr Greer is the Director of the Center for the Study of Extra-Terrestrial Intelligence (CSETI) in Denver, Colorado.

'In July 1992 my friend, Annick Nevejan and I decided to visit Wiltshire for a short holiday and possibly to see some crop formations. We arrived in Alton Barnes the day after the formation of the Snail and decided to stay for further developments.

'I had become interested in crop formations as an extension to my interest in prehistoric archaeology – there was the obvious link between

Figure 74: Formation at Galteemore Farm, Beckhampton, Wiltshire, July 1992. Wheat. © Jürgen Kronig

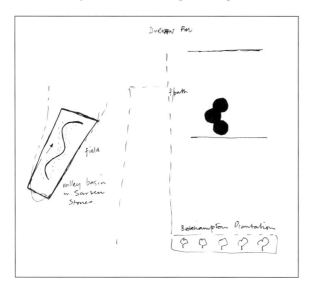

Figure 75: A drawing of the event at Galteemore Farm. © Chris Mansell

formations and existing sites. Annick, however, had never seen a crop formation and was quite excited to see the Snail. Over the following days we visited a number of formations as they were reported to us.

'On the afternoon of 16 July, at about 5.30 p.m., we located the triple ring formation at Galteemore Farm, near Beckhampton plantation. We had not entered the formation and were looking across the valley towards Hemp Knoll. It was a fairly windy day with periods of hazy sunshine. While looking across the valley we noticed that a mist had formed above a fallow field next to an area of sarsen stones. The mist seemed to be floating at a constant height above the field and moving north-east. However, at the same time it seemed to be confined to that particular field. Annick moved along the footpath to observe it from a different angle and during this time it appeared to form itself into a serpent-like shape with a coiled tail. Then it slowly disintegrated.

'About a week later we were sitting at an adjacent table to a group of American visitors to the area who were discussing crop formations. Eventually we started to compare notes and they showed us a formation that had appeared the previous day and which they had observed from the air. This was exactly the same shape as the one that appeared in the mist, near Beckhampton, a week earlier.

'The American visitors formed part of a group from CSETI. They asked us to accompany them the following day to visit some formations to exchange ideas and discuss our individual involvement. As a result of our meeting, Steve

[Greer] invited us to join their project concerning active communication with extra-terrestrial intelligence and with the agency concerned with the manufacture of the crop formations. Their research involved group meditation and concentration using varying images and ciphers, plus the use of high-powered hand-held searchlights to convey simple shapes into the sky.

'On the evening of Saturday 26 July, at about 11.30 p.m., Annick and I arrived at the crop formation near Tawsmead Copse, West Stowell, where the project was based for that evening. As we arrived it started to rain heavily and before we could join the rest of the party they were already coming out of the formation.

'After some discussion we decided to leave the track and return to the concrete road south-west of Woodborough Hill, since we had heard that cars sometimes got stuck in the mud. The whole party parked in a lay-by on the right-hand side of the road facing towards the Woodborough barns [away from Alton Barnes]. After further discussion it was decided to abandon the project for that evening.

'A little later, at approximately 12.10 a.m., two members of the CSETI team returned to their hotel as they had to leave early the next day. This left Annick and myself in my car and two CSETI members (Steve and Dr Sandra Small) in a car immediately in front of us.

'The weather had cleared up slightly but occasional patches of drizzle were still coming and going so, after a short conversation, we decided to wait a further five to ten minutes before leaving. Annick and I were sitting in my car talking about the evening's events. I had opened the driver's window from which I noticed, towards what I estimated to be the south, a long strip of coloured lights. These appeared to be revolving from left to right, changing colour from red through white to green. Having never seen anything like this before, I got out of the car and went to tell Steve. He opened his window, saw the lights and immediately recognized it as what he called a "non-terrestrial craft".

'By this time we were all out on the road watching the "craft" as it moved slowly from east to west and became stationary at a position just above the horizon. This all took about three to five minutes as the lights moved very slowly.

'We estimated that it must have been 1,500 to 2,500 feet [455–758m] away by noting the positions of street lights and electricity pylons. At one point we also saw it partially disappear behind some trees so we could say that at its point of origination it must have been very low. Steve estimated that the "craft" must have been 80 to 100 feet [24–30] in diameter.

'It occurred to me later that the lights simply appeared and weren't seen travelling towards that point. It also struck me that at a certain stage in its movement it appeared to illuminate (possibly by reflection from the ground) its own structure and we all saw that it was a cigar-shaped object, possibly circular seen from the edge, with a small projection at the top [see Figure 76].

'As the "craft" became stationary I thought it flipped through 90 degrees so that we could see its underside. The light formation was now triangular with a triangle of three amber lights at the top and a row of coloured lights forming the base of the triangle, again ranging from red at the left, to blue-green at the right. The lights on the underbelly were much dimmer than those viewed from the side.

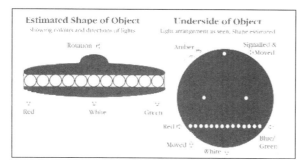

Figure 76: Diagram of the Woodborough Hill UFO.
© Chris Mansell

'After a few moments one of the orange lights forming the upper triangle seemed to separate from the formation, move slightly west and return to the formation. Then one of the red lights at the base of the formation also seemed to separate, move slightly to the east and rejoin the formation. Next it appeared that three red lights broke away from the formation, moved a considerable distance to the west and then rejoined the formation. During the whole of this time, about ten minutes, we were observing these events through binoculars and making an audio tape of events on a portable cassette recorder. There was no doubt at all about what was happening.

'We were all fairly excited but managed to keep a careful watch on events as they unfolded. The "craft" was completely silent and during the time span over which we witnessed this occurrence a

number of cars were seen and heard passing by on the road (the A342) beyond where the "craft" was situated. There was also an Army helicopter which could be heard in the distance but not seen.

'Steve decided that he would like to try to communicate with the object and asked Dr Small to take one of the high-powered hand-held lights from the back of his car while we kept the craft under observation. He pointed the light directly at the formation and signalled two short bursts. To our amazement the light at the top of the formation mirrored this signal exactly. This procedure was repeated a number of times and on each occasion the single light flashed back in exactly the same pattern.

'The "craft" started to move away to the west and then to the south, and appeared to be going down the Avon Valley. We finally lost sight of it and that terminated the encounter. The time span of the whole event was about 15 minutes.

'During the course of this event many attempts were made to obtain accurate compass bearings of the points of origin and disappearance of the object. However, on each occasion we tried, the compass was found to be giving a completely different result. (Positions were measured accurately the following day after careful consideration had been given to physical land form and structures – Woodborough Hill, Alton Barns, Woodborough Bridge and so on.)

'Shortly afterwards, two other people stopped in their car and reported to us that at some point during this time span they had seen the Tawsmead field illuminated in a strange fashion. It was a cloudy night and there was no moon, stars or local street lighting. The field appeared to be lit by some unseen source for just about 30 seconds, which then faded away leaving just the blackness of the wet and starless night.

'We stood for some considerable time discussing these events, ensuring that we all had a clear picture of what had happened. At about 1.20 to 1.30 a.m., while looking almost directly east, a similar object seemed to come towards us but not nearly as close. This object disappeared towards the south and was completely silent. We estimated this to be at a distance of one to two miles [1.5–3km]. Eventually we decided to return home as the weather was worsening and planned to meet the next day.

'On 30 July it was noted that a small crop circle, approximately 40 feet [12m] in diameter, was found in wheat at OS map reference SU115607, near Woodborough Bridge (over the Kennett and Avon Canal), in the close vicinity of where the sighting had originated. There had never previously been circles in this area near Woodborough.

'I am apprehensive about making any firm statement concerning the involvement of the event that we witnessed with the manufacture of crop formations. However, it would certainly appear through our and other sightings around this time, that the possibility of a link exists. It seems just too coincidental that the group from the CSETI should be using the crop formation platform and it resulting in the events that we witnessed. I have not experienced anything like this before or since.'

Crop Circles and UFO 'Nests'

Ron Gaist, a Sydney television executive, took aerial photographs of a diamond-shaped clearing in a sugar cane field near Tully. A Queensland University study failed to find any explanation for the way the cane stalks had been pulled out by the roots and swirled into a mat about ten metres across, indicating the movement of some object. Whirlwinds were discounted as a possible cause (they tend to move in straight lines), and so were crocodiles, 'the "nest" being too neat'.

When Ron's film was developed a 'bank of lights' appeared on several of the shots, which were not visible while the photographs were being taken. They were not due to a fault of the camera, because they did not appear on the rest of the film or in photographs taken before or since. Ron also discounted the possibility that the markings were caused by sand ridges in the cane fields: 'Sand ridges don't run in geometric patterns.' Ron believes that he has uncovered new evidence of strange aerial phenomena in Queensland's famed 'flying saucer' belt, and would now like someone to tell him just what it is that he has photographed!

There is an Aboriginal legend that one of their gods, Chic-ah-Bunnah, sped through the air emitting a dazzling blue light. He also ate glowing red coals and took off from the earth with a frightening bang and a roaring sound! Unlike all the other Aboriginal gods, Chic-ah-Bunnah symbolized no other known living thing, but was shaped like a man.

Language and Communication

Are crop circles a form of communication from another world? Are their shapes and patterns meant to tell us something? Some people, such as American researcher Ron Russell, believe this to be the case.

Ron Russell has been playing an increasingly active role investigating the crop circle phenomenon. He began in the late 1980s after being struck by the circles' strange beauty. From an early age he had been fascinated by reports of strange ships in the sky. He often used to ask himself: 'What if we are not alone? What if there are others visiting us?'

As with all mysteries, one question leads on to another. 'How do they communicate their knowledge? I speculated that they might have created symbols and writing that might be marvellously different from ours.' The crop formations, swirled into such beautiful and controlled shapes, struck Ron as possibly being 'the language for which I had been looking'.

In 1992 Ron joined the research team, led by Steve Greer from CSETI, which was visiting various crop circles in Southern England (see above).

Figure 77: Tawsmead Copse, West Stowell, Wiltshire, July 1992. Wheat. © Jürgen Kronig

'On a beautiful, cold, star-filled English summer night, July 24 1992, the CSETI team met near Marlborough, Wiltshire, at a private farm. We had been given permission to visit a hidden crop circle and ring formation near woods on the north-west edge of the farm. It was in a slight dip in the field and was not visible from any vantage point except by air [see Figure 77].

'We found the formation by starlight after walking from our caravan of cars parked some distance away. Six of us first entered the circle from the East and crossed it to go into the ring. On entering the ring we set down our cameras and high-powered signal lights, and gathered in a group to quieten our minds and bond our spirits. We were on a CSETI skywatch, so we prepared ourselves for the strong possibility of a close encounter.

'Sharon, our CSETI field director in Denver, led our group in a short prayer and we meditated in silence for 20 minutes. I felt an urge to walk and explore, and get the feel of the formation. I rose and whispered to Sharon that I needed to stretch my legs and would be gone only a minute. Some of the others were still deep in meditation.

'I set out to my right, walking counter-clockwise along the lay of the flattened wheat, following a path that seemed to be 10 feet [3m] wide. The time was about 11 p.m. and it was a moonless night. I had no flashlight and could see only a short distance in front of me. I could see the edges of the formation where the crop was still standing.

'Though not an athlete, I am a reasonably healthy middle-aged man. Normally I can hike many miles easily without fatigue, so I was somewhat surprised to find myself exerting a lot of effort and having to breathe deeply as I plodded forward. The pathway was becoming steep and as I climbed I wondered why it had been made on the side of a hill. I hadn't heard of any of the glyphs appearing on a hill before, but I was new to this research. The path soon became even steeper. I noticed how quiet it was and how "thick" the minutes had become. I wondered if the weather had changed during my climb. After a few minutes of uphill hiking, leaning my body forward into the hill to prevent slipping, I reached a plateau and stopped for a minute to catch my breath. It was lighter there and I could see better.

'The air moved slowly and felt "dense" somehow. I wondered again why this formation had been made on the side of a hill and why anyone would have planted wheat here in the first place. It would be difficult to plant on a slope like this. The slope was so great that any tractor would have fallen over. Puzzled, I continued on around the ring.

'The path curved off to my left and seemed wider than it had on the uphill climb. I moved more briskly now, determined to rejoin the team since I was concerned that I had been gone too long. The path began to descend gradually. I found that I now had to lean back and be careful of my footing since the laid wheat was so slippery. The descent was time-consuming. My knees felt

weak and my heart rate escalated with the muscle tension and stress of my descent.

'This was even harder than the climb up. I proceeded ahead for what seemed like five minutes before I came to what felt like a flat area. Far in the distance I could hear someone talking. After another minute or so of walking I arrived at the place from where I had started and rejoined the group. I told Sharon that I was sorry I had been gone so long, but that this formation was evidently quite large and very steep, and I was tired from my walk. I could see surprise on her face as I said this.

"Wait a minute, Ron. This is flat ground and by all I've heard it's only about 70 feet [21m] in diameter. You've only been gone a minute, as you said you'd be."

"No. That can't be," I argued. "I almost slipped on the hill and I got tired, too – I'm not kidding."

'Sharon disagreed with me and said she would walk around it herself to see. Though I felt it had taken me more than 10 minutes to walk the formation, she was gone for only 30 seconds or so.

"It's just a flat ring," she reported.

'I felt shock at hearing this and began to wonder whether my experience was real. Sharon was correct, of course. The next day, when I visited the circle and ring in the sunlight, I was startled by how small the ring was. There was no hill anywhere nearby that could account for my experience, though I knew I had stayed in the ring path. So I had climbed an uphill. Or one that was there only for when I was. The crop circles, "symbols" of the language I had been seeking, seemed to have been imprinted right into my feet, my physiology and my breath. The experience

Figure 78: Cherhill White Horse and monument

dramatically altered my understanding of the word "communication".'

More Communication?

In 1993 Ron returned to Wiltshire, and on 27 July, he and other CSETI researchers visited the Furze Knoll hillside near Calne. Gradually they became aware of a low, steady persistent drone, which the group likened to a squadron of stationary Second World War heavy bombers a mile or so away.

Eventually it was decided that Ron and another of the group, Mark Briggs, should go and investigate the sound.

'It was about 11.30 p.m. and, as we left, the wind had eased up a bit. It was quite dark as we walked across the field away from the group and towards

Marconi's Towers. We came to the fence enclosing the base of the towers and circled around due north-east. After five minutes of brisk walking we came to the edge of the hilltop. We looked down on the valley below the Cherhill White Horse.

'We could see the lights of Cherhill and, further east, Compton Bassett and Calne. We looked ahead towards the sound (about 500 yards [455m] to the north-east) and saw a double row of 20 or so lights. Slowly a large craft rose from the midst of the lights.

"Look, Mark," I said. "It looks like a space ship."

"Wow!" Mark replied. "I see it all right, but it doesn't sound right . . . "

'I had to agree. It sounded like a big World War

II prop bomber and seemed to be taking off from some airstrip near Cherhill.'

After some discussion and obsvervation of the craft through binoculars, Ron and Mark reluctantly came to the conclusion that it was, in fact, an old vintage airplane, rather than a flying saucer, and dejectedly reported this back to the rest of the group.

Still uneasy about the 'airplane', the next day Ron drove round the Cherhill area trying to find the airstrip from where such a plane would have to take off. The countryside was rural farmland with small cottages all around.

'From where could a plane – if it was a plane – have taken off? I looked around for hours and travelled up every road in the area, and could find no feasible spot for any sort of airplane. In subsequent days I searched an ever-widening area for a location from which a large prop vintage aircraft could have flown. I could never find one. I went over to Yatesbury, some miles distance, where an old World War II airbase had been, but it was totally wrecked and there was no strip, no lights, just farmland in crops.'

A week or so later, Ron was travelling towards Bath on the main A4 road.

'It was on 9 August, early morning, when I was driving from Marlborough to Bath on the A4 past Cherhill when I thought I had gone past the area where the mystery flight had taken place. As I rounded the bend, WOW! There was a huge crop formation, 425 feet [129m] long, right in the area

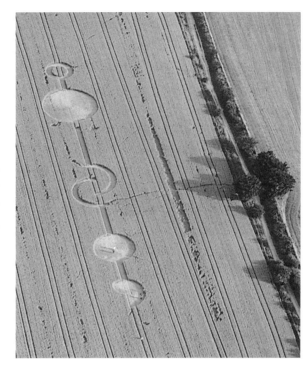

Figure 79: 'Hand of Friendship', Cherhill, near Calne, Wiltshire, 7 August 1993, length 360 ft (109m). Wheat

where we had seen the ship! I thought this to be a strange coincidence indeed. I stopped and photographed the beautiful, virgin formation. And again the rational mind won. What else could this be but a coincidence?

'A month after I had returned home to Denver, Peter Sorenson and Busty Taylor reported a second mysterious formation in that same field, one that had all the earmarks of a "saucer nest" or UFO landing site. The rocks were unusually magnetized, a peculiar orange dust covered the area, and although the wheat field had been harvested, a shape could clearly be seen embossed in the stubble remaining. It had obviously been there for some time.'

Was the slow, heavy plane really a UFO, adapting itself into a form that might be acceptable to the observer, thereby not causing alarm or distress? Was there a connection between the Cherhill formation and Ron's experience? Had the plane or its occupants been instrumental in leaving a complex 'slow release' pattern in the field? Ron is convinced that he and Mark had witnessed something in that field, and had failed to realize its significance.

Sticky Trails

The orange powder left on the ground in the stubble near Cherhill is very reminiscent of the grey sticky powder covering the ground that André Tong reported as long ago as 1965. (*See Chapter 1 for more of André's experiences.*)

During the first week in May 1965, André Tong, his father, mother and a workman had been working at a farm in Warwickshire for two weeks, frame-grafting fruit trees.

'One evening, we decided to go for an evening meal. We left the orchard at about 7 p.m. and came back at 10 p.m., had some coffee and retired to bed. At about 1 a.m., the caravan in which we were sleeping started to vibrate. This went on for about ten minutes then it stopped for about five minutes. Then the caravan started to rock from side to side, very gently to start with, then very wildly. All the things in the caravan were thrown about. We were thrown from side to side and my mother had her face cut. This went on for about 20 minutes, then it stopped. We were all very frightened. I got up and looked out of the door; there was not a sound to be heard but I could see about 50 lights made up of three colours – red, blue and white. They were a little bit smaller than the size of a football, and they all seemed to be the same distance apart. They appeared to be all around me.

'This went on for a further two hours, then the vibration and the rocking started again, before finally all went still. We tried to clear up the mess, without going outside.

'In the morning, as soon as it was light, we went outside to check on any damage. While the caravan had been rocking from side to side it had obviously hit our car, and both were damaged. There was a fine grey powder, which was very sticky, all over everything. It took a long time to wash the car and caravan.

'When we went to work that morning, we found all our scions [grafted cuttings] on the trees had gone. There was a circle formation, the same as the apple crop [*see pages 6–7*], and the scions that had been sucked out were all from within the circle. It took us four days to replace them. The affected area encompassing the trees, caravan, road and meadow formed a large circle. The meadow behind the caravan was also covered in the grey powder, as was the road and fence.'

What force could have created such devastation and what was the origin of this strange sticky, grey powder? André wonders whether anything happened to him or if 'they' did anything to him that night in Warwickshire, as he has experienced feelings of *déjà vu* ever since.

Chapter Nine

Conclusion

O day and night, but this is wondrous strange!
There are more things in heaven and earth,
Horatio, than are dreamt of in your philosphy.
Hamlet I, 5

As researcher and investigator of the paranormal from childhood, and deeply interested in investigating the crop circle phenomenon since 1989, I have been repeatedly asked, 'When are you going to write about the strange and mysterious things happening to people in the crop fields?'

Throughout this book I have tried to be as objective as possible; not an easy task when inundated with so many extraordinary events occurring to seemingly ordinary people. That strange things appear to be happening, not only around the crop circles, but in every aspect of our lives, there is no doubt, and as more and more stories come to light, it seems as though certain mechanisms act as catalysts for yet even more unaccountable happenings.

Many kind people have telephoned or sent me reports. Written accounts are preferable for we are all individuals and each of us has a unique and special way of expressing ourselves, giving the 'flavour' of the experience that is of the essence.

All the accounts in this book have been carefully examined and followed up personally. A great deal of time has been taken in making and verifying the selection. It has been an intriguing and rewarding experience and I have met many charming and fascinating people in the course of my investigations. Their accounts testify to the strange physical and psychological effects crop circles have on people and animals, not to mention the effects they have on machinery. They also convey the strange and beautiful geometric complexities of the formations, which are surely beyond the capabilities of humans to create in the time that the formations appear.

It seems obvious that something out of the ordinary is happening. The questions we have to ask ourselves are 'What?' 'Why?' and 'How?'

I often look back to my first crop circle 'experience' on a sunny day in July 1990: I sat in a circle with a severely damaged shoulder (*see Chapter 3, pages 27–30*); when I left the circle my shoulder was completely healed. Was I hallucinating? Definitely not. I had witnesses with me.

I believe there are too many things happening in and around the crop fields that simply cannot be explained away by any logical mind process. Can a distinction be made between mind suspension and loss of time, or are we exploring aspects of the same field? Are UFO sightings simply aeroplanes or other explainable lights?

Over the centuries we have witnessed quantum leaps of understanding and knowledge. Some of these great thinkers were so far ahead of their time – Copernicus, Galileo, Leonardo da Vinci, to name but three – that their findings threatened the teaching and very order of their day.

This book has encompassed many areas, not just of human involvement but the curious behaviour of birds and animals whilst inside or in the vicinity of crop circles, and bizarre mechanical failures as well. Why do some camera, mobile telephone and pocket computer batteries drain away instantly? Why do airplane compasses swing wildly when passing over certain crop formations? Is there any connection between the crash of a light aircraft and the night a crop circle appeared? Why do dogs start to howl on nights when formations appear, and why won't they go into the circles?

What happened to all the apples that disappeared from a heavily-laden tree the night a formation appeared? The tree was stripped bare of fruit and no trace was left of the fruit nor any twigs, leaves or branches on the ground anywhere near the apple tree. Why are there so many luminous sightings associated with the crop circles? What are these 'luminosities'?

Some of these occurrences, of course, can be explained away quite easily, but others cannot. So what is happening? What is the answer? Are the crop circles acting as 'gateways' to other dimensions and other realities? Are we seeing evidence of parallel worlds? I believe the answer is 'YES', and that these are points that deserve close scrutiny.

Is there a common link to all crop circle events? Keith Wakelam, a retired electronics engineer (and author of *Discovering Eternity*), suggests that the connecting link could be:

'A mysterious force invoked by nature or by the human mind, sometimes producing subtle changes in the thoughts of those it seeks out. A force which can be impressed upon the environment to produce fields which persist for long periods – like the horizontal effects of energy lines or vertical whirlpools of energy in buildings. These effects can be augmented, tapped or nullified, using what seems to be magical practices or devices.

'A force which can act through the human sympathetic nervous system to confer psychic abilities, like dowsing, can in other cases cause healing, in others to produce changes of moods, fear, discomfort and actual pain, memory loss, distortion of time sense, dreams, visions and hallucinations.

'A force which acts upon plants and animals, which sometimes apports physical objects and causes other mysterious changes in the environment, which defy rational explanation.'

Leonardo da Vinci and James Lovelock, as well as primitive people going back to the dawn of our existence, believed that the planet was a living, breathing organism, interacting and inter-relating with all living matter. Da Vinci, in his 72-page *Codex* manuscript (compiled around 1506–1510), attributes the ebb and flow of the tides to the 'breathing of this terrestrial machine', identifying it with the lungs. He also writes, 'We might say that the earth has a spirit of growth, that its flesh is the soil, its bones the arrangement and connection of the rocks of which the mountains are composed, its cartilage the tufa, and its blood the springs of water.'

Malcolm Stewart, geometer and lecturer in Cultural History, suggests that if you expand that idea, the cosmos is fundamentally conscious and has a field of information that is self-aware, with circulating transmissions of information. The Gaia Principle of the earth is one of homoeostasis, retaining the biosphere in a state of balance.

Stewart believes that what we are dealing with is a question of *scale*:

'Imagine yourself the size of a single cell within your body. You might look around you at the processes going on and – because you would be so small they may appear to you to be simply a matter of mechanistic push/pull actors such as gravity, momentum and electricity. But actually the processes are alive. It's just a question of scale. So we, at our actual size, look out at the vast cosmos and interpret its activity in a mechanistic way… whereas it too may well be alive – with life processes too huge for us to appreciate. Our own fundamental experience tells us "I am alive, I am conscious"; prior to that we don't know anything and maybe we do not know much after that, the rest is largely opinion rather than fact.

'Why is it that those two primary pieces of information are never included in the description of the cosmos by the physicists? In trying to describe the nature of the unified field they call on the electromagnetic force, the strong force, the weak force, and gravity. Are enough forces included? It would seem that the whole cosmos is alive and conscious. If one takes that perspective, then matter and material energies are being precipitated out of a field of different order.'

I believe an argument, if properly tendered, is eligible for debate, whether the reader reaches the same conclusions as the author or not. It stimulates much needed discussion and readers must judge the weight of argument for themselves.

For many people there is a big problem with anything unknown or unexplainable. Maybe the circles are not all of human origin? Maybe the circles are not all formed by atmospheric conditions? For those people who find this threatening, the claims of hoaxers are a blessing in disguise. They act as a safety net for all who fear what their rational minds cannot explain.

Yet how can the hoaxers explain away the famous 17th-century woodcut of the Mowing Devil? Or reports of circles that were seen in the 1920s, 1930s and 1940s? Or the strange feelings and strange happenings experienced by people over the years? Are we all first-class fabricators or victims of over-developed mythical imagery?

Notwithstanding these claims, sufficient evidence has been accumulated to suggest that scientific research into this phenomenon should continue, for there is no completely satisfactory explanation. The deeper the investigations, the deeper the mystery.

Might Terry Pratchett have a point in his delightful *Lords and Ladies* when he tells us that:

> At circle time, when the walls between this and that are thinner, when there are all sorts of leakages … Ah, then choices are made, then the universe can be sent careening down a different leg of the well-known Trousers of time … Crop circles burst like raindrops … splat!… They appear when the walls between realities get weaker … You'd be able to walk from one universe to another.

Could a dear deceased friend, Kathy Wakelam, have hit upon the solution when she suggested that there could be more than seeds planted in the fields! Something like a piece of DNA in a virus, which infects the crop and replicates itself throughout the area of the circle. The DNA can contain a pattern, as each of our cells contains the pattern of our whole body.

In the same way as spores in the ground produce patterns (fairy rings), which expand in a circular fashion as microbes would on a Petri Dish – more circles appearing as they continue to propagate themselves – it might be suggested that particles whose pattern could have been imprinted in the ground in miniature, as a viral DNA coding, might behave in a similar fashion, and having been ingested by the seed, become part of the crop.

The virus would remain undetected until the crop was ripening and then some event would trigger a chain reaction, so that the crop would fall in the designated pattern. The change in the DNA of the crop would be so minute, only sufficient to produce a bending in the stalk, that it could remain undetected.

What would happen to us when we ate the genetically modified grain? Time alone will tell what these and other man-made genetic alterations will do to us! Someone could be programming us. To what end?

Legend tells us that Apollonius of Tyana (who was born about four years before the start of the Christian era), a philosopher and initiate of the Inner Teachings, was given talismans which, during his widespread travels, he buried at certain chosen places around the world. In due course and at the appropriate time, these consecrated spots would be activated and utilized as centres of importance. Could the imprints of the crop circles be present in the ground and is the time now right for their manifestation by some external force?

Another theory was put to me by Keith Wakelam: could someone be transmitting from the moon? On the face of it, this sounds pretty implausible, but he suggests that:

> 'Microwaves might be favoured by entities transmitting to us from outside the Earth. They are of lower energy than light and pass easily through the Earth's atmosphere, i.e. they require the least energy to transmit.
>
> 'They might choose a moment when the moon was in darkness, a new moon, and the sun behind

them, to transmit for greater contrast. Or, if they wished to remain undetected, they might wish to transmit during daytime or at full moon, when their particular transmission would be masked by the rocks around them, so that you would hardly notice it against the background.

'The degree of spread from 30–300 feet [9–90m] is typically what you would expect of a laser beam from the moon. Getting in the way of a microwave beam at this range would be unpleasant, but not fatal, as it would be if shorter, higher beams were used. They have to be able to see with a certain amount of accuracy a particular area of the Earth's surface which they couldn't do very well from, say, Mars or Jupiter. They would need to be sufficiently close in and it is unlikely that they would be making use of radiant energies as they would be too faint at that distance. The transmission time would play a part; from the distance of Jupiter it is 15–30 minutes and so it would make it very difficult to "hit" an area with any accuracy as the earth is rotating at about 500 miles [805km] an hour at this latitude. They could easily be miles out!'

The point about this particular theory is that so many of the crop formations are found in such remote and obscure locations that they would go unnoticed unless they were spotted from the air. The full beauty of the complex design can also only be seen to full advantage from the air.

Take the Nazca Lines in the Peruvian Andes photographed in 1973 by Skylab–2 astronauts, for a similar example. This network of straight lines is interspersed with giant standing objects. Due to the area covered and the structured pattern, it is clear that they were placed there for some purpose, the trace-work being neither random nor accidental. It has been widely suggested that this was a landing strip for ancient astronauts.

The Nazca Lines are only part of the picture, for there is more aerial evidence of giant carvings and petroglyphs which can only be seen properly from above, as with the crop formations. There are enormous petroglyphs of birds, insects and people. Were these ground traces used as identifying features for landing space craft? Could that hold true today?

That there appears to be no ready solution to the crop circles, no simple answer, does not mean that one will not be found. Consider the developments which have occurred within a relatively short span of time – discoveries which would have been ridiculed just a few years ago. Inventions and discoveries frequently happen by chance. Take Columbus and the 'discovery' of America in 1492: he and his crew were trying to find the westen route to India. Moving into more recent times, John Logie Baird, the inventor of the infra-red camera, happened upon the concept of television by accident. Working in conjunction with Sir Oliver Lodge, investigating life after death and the possibility of using the infra-red camera to assist with communication in this field, he conceived the idea of transmitting pictures by wireless waves – 'seeing by wireless' – in 1923.

A large measure of scientific understanding of crop circles is beginning to emerge, which will be written up in a later publication.

However, in the meantime can we really dismiss the historical evidence of 'ancient' knowledge and wisdom? Are the ancient Egyptians, the Babylonians, the Chinese and others who did wonderful 'new' things, the remnants of the 'Atlantean' civilization? Can we discount the story handed down by Critias and recorded by Plato? (*Atlantis: Myth or Reality*, Murray Hope). Around 7,000 years ago simultaneous developments in apparently unconnected places occurred. It was the Egyptians and the Babylonians who were the first to inscribe stones, bones and clay tablets with symbols and simple pictures; who established trading routes 5,000 years ago, having invented wind-powered sailing ships; who in 3500BC developed weights and measures and invented scales; and who, with the Chinese, in 1300BC were the first to use ink. Were they the gods and goddesses of old, or were they privy to some special knowledge brought by others?

> Deities have appeared in forms so visible that they have compelled everyone, who is not senseless or hardened in impiety, to confess the presence of the Gods.
>
> (Cicero, *Of the Nature of the Gods*.)

I wonder if those ancient people would have had an explanation for the crop circles? I suspect they might. For, indeed, I believe that part of the answer will be found in the natural world, portrayed in the form of a new understanding of maths, physics and medicine; knowledge that was already recognized intellectually and intuitively by our dim and distant ancestors but later lost to us. Until comparatively recently little progress had been made in mechanical, technical and scientific knowledge. However, in overall terms, the picture looks slightly different and would indicate a rapid acceleration of knowledge.

How have we achieved this? Alvin Toffler (in his book *Future Shock*) relates how Kenneth Boulding, an eminent economist, observed, 'Almost as much has happened since I was born as happened before.'

Toffler suggests that 'plotted on a graph, the line representing progress in the past generation would leap vertically off the page'. Thanks to the 'snowball effect' of progress (with the advance of technology, scooping up existing knowledge, carrying it with it and gathering speed and momentum all the while), millions of years can go by and then suddenly there is an explosion of knowledge.

Have crop circles got a part to play in this universal theatre? Can they be dismissed unilaterally as products of wishful thinking? Are they all man-made? Are the artists little green men, as some would have us believe? That the whole subject is prone to ridicule has long been an accepted penalty all serious researchers have had to accept. However, crop circle researchers are by no means alone, for all those who are at the cutting edge of any new concept are aware that this is all part of the package. This is by no means an isolated case. Research into cold nuclear fusion is just such an example, with most scientists deciding that researchers' claims about this were not justified. However, none other than the Japanese car manufacturers, Toyota, is providing substantial amounts of finance to further exploration in Switzerland, so someone must obviously believe that there is potential in the process!

When the crop circle 'energy' has been decoded, what will it reveal? Can we draw a parallel between these two phenomena? It would indeed seem possible to do so, *for as yet there is no proof, but neither have they been disproved.* The jury is out!

How long will the shapes continue to adorn our fields? Have they got a message for us, or is it romantic, fanciful thinking? It seems to me that the circles will be with us and will continue to evolve just as long as we continue to focus on them. Just as the one hundredth monkey syndrome illustrates how the cumulative pooled memory of a species can profoundly influence the behaviour of all subsequent members of that species, once the transmission has been received and the connection established.

For the full answer however, I believe we may have to look to areas of wider consciousness that can bypass normal thought. Einstein tells us, 'there comes a time when the mind reaches a higher plane of knowledge but can never prove how it got there'. I believe we cannot dismiss the possibility of some external intelligence being involved in this phenomenon.

I have but one request of the reader . . . be open-minded.

Key to Silhouettes

The 1980s

A   Cheesefoot Head, Hampshire, 1981
B   Goodworth Clatford, Hampshire, 1985
C   Wantage, Oxfordshire, 1986
D   Cheesefoot Head, Hampshire, 1986
E   Corhampton, Hampshire, 1988
F   Bishops Canning, Wiltshire, 1988
G   East Kennett, Wiltshire, 1988
H   Silbury Hill, Wiltshire, 1988
I   Longwood, Hampshire, 1989
J   Cherhill, Wiltshire, 1989
K   Winterbourne Stoke, Wiltshire, 1989

1990

A   Bishops Canning, Wiltshire
B   Etchilhampton, Wiltshire
C   Fawley Down, Hampshire
D   Alton Barnes, Wiltshire
E   East Kennett, Wiltshire
F   Stanton St Bernard, Wiltshire
G   Amersham, Buckinghamshire
H   Litchfield, Hampshire
I   Chilcomb, Hampshire
J   Westbury, Wiltshire
K   Fawley Down, Hampshire

1991

A   Froxfield, Wiltshire
B   Cheesefoot Head, Hampshire

C   Chilcomb, Hampshire
D   Froxfield, Wiltshire
E   Newton St Loe, Avon
F   Froxfield, Wiltshire
G   Preschute Down, Wiltshire
H   East Kennett, Wiltshire
I   Alton Priors, Wiltshire
J   Barbury Castle, Wiltshire
K   Ickleton, Cambridgeshire

1992

A   Alton Barnes, Wiltshire
B   Airmyn, Yorkshire
C   Berry Pomeroy, Devon
D   Froxfield, Wiltshire
E   Lockeridge, Wiltshire
F   West Stowell, Wiltshire
G   Tidcombe, Hampshire
H   Silbury Hill, Wiltshire
I   Ogbourne St George, Wiltshire
J   Silbury Hill, Wiltshire
K   Alton Barnes, Wiltshire
L   West Stowell (Tawsmead Copse), Wiltshire

1993

A   Windmill Hill, Wiltshire
B   Shoreham, Sussex
C   Nuneaton, Warwickshire
D   Bythorn, Cambridgeshire
E   Loughborough, Leicestershire

1994

A   Alton Barnes, Wiltshire

B	Silbury Hill, Wiltshire
C	Bishops Canning, Wiltshire
D	Wilsford, Wiltshire
E	Hackpen Hill, Wiltshire
F	Froxfield, Wiltshire
G	Barton Stacey, Hampshire

1995

A	Danebury Hillfort, Hampshire
B	West Meon, Hampshire
C	Wilmington, Sussex
D	Longwood, Hampshire
E	Alresford, Hampshire
F	Kingsclere, Hampshire

1996

A	Alton Barnes, Wiltshire
B	Littlebury Green, Essex
C	Martock, Somerset
D	Liddington Castle, Wiltshire
E	Stonehenge, Wiltshire

1997

A	Barbury Castle, Wiltshire
B	Barbury Castle, Wiltshire
C	Winterbourne Bassett, Wiltshire
D	Cuxton, Kent
E	Olivers Castle, Wiltshire
F	Etchilhampton, Wiltshire
G	Silbury Hill, Wiltshire
H	Alton Priors, Wiltshire
I	Strethall, Essex
J	Littlebury Green, Essex

1998

A	Weyhill, Hampshire
B	Silbury Hill, Wiltshire
C	Goodworth Clatford, Hampshire
D	Newton St Loe, Avon
E	Marlborough, Wiltshire
F	Chiseldon, Wiltshire
G	Newton St Loe, Avon
H	Chiseldon, Wiltshire
I	East Kennett, Wiltshire
J	East Kennett, Wiltshire
K	Trowbridge, Wiltshire
L	West Overton, Wiltshire
M	Trowbridge, Wiltshire
N	Winterbourne Bassett, Wiltshire

A	West Overton, Wiltshire
B	Avebury Avenue, Wiltshire
C	West Overton, Wiltshire
D	North Down, Bishops Canning, Wiltshire
E	Beckhampton, Wiltshire
F	West Meon, Hampshire
G	Avebury Trusloe, Wiltshire
H	West Overton, Wiltshire
I	Cuxton, Kent
J	East Kennett, Wiltshire
K	The Wansdyke, Wiltshire
L	Clatford, Wiltshire
M	Chiseldon, Wiltshire

A	Yatesbury, Wiltshire
B	Avebury, Wiltshire
C	Avebury, Wiltshire
D	Beckhampton, Wiltshire
E	Avebury, Wiltshire
F	Dadford, Buckinghamshire

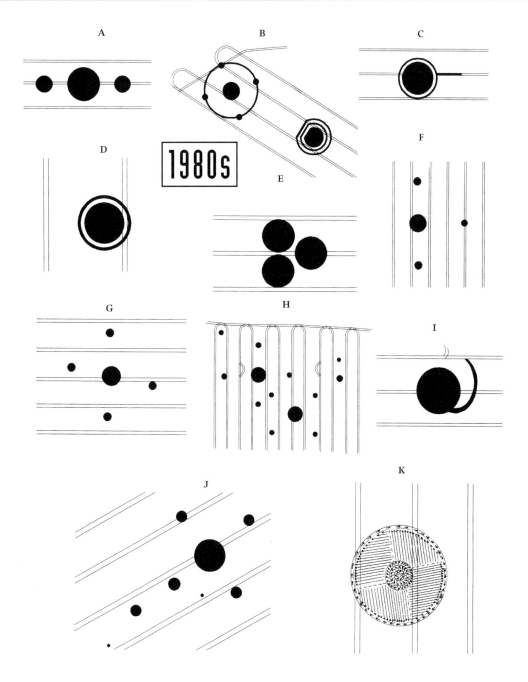

A

B

C

1980s

D

E

F

G

H

I

J

K

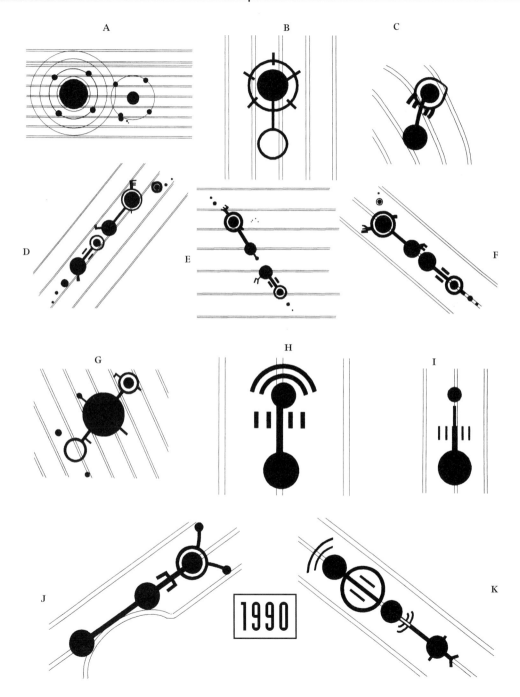

A

B

C

D

E

F

G

H

I

J

1990

K

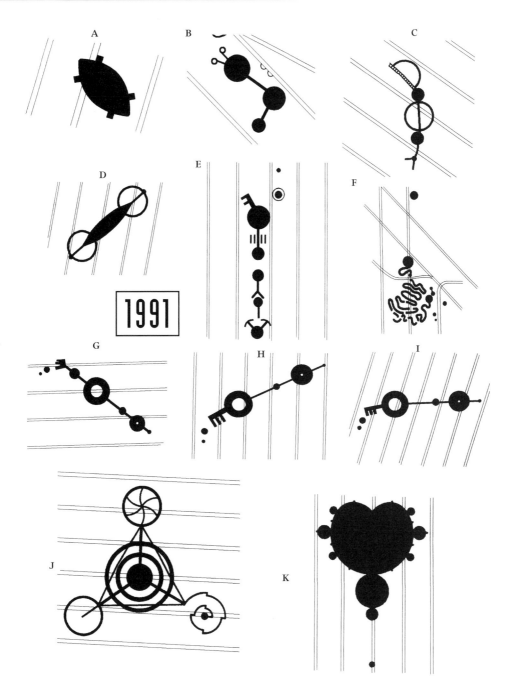

A

B

C

D

E

1991

F

G

H

I

J

K

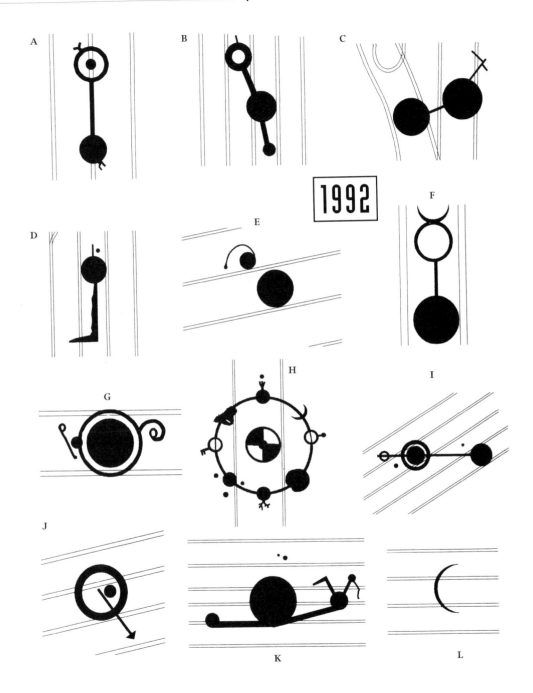

A

B

C

1992

E

F

D

G

H

I

J

K

L

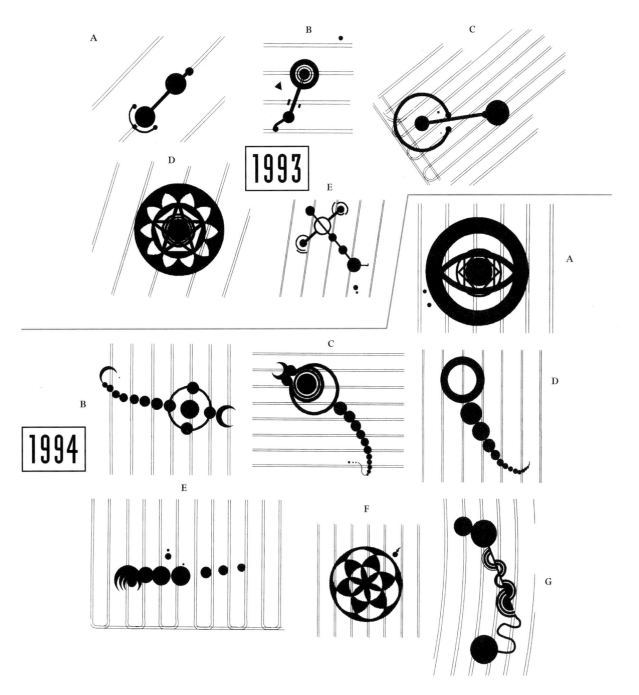

A

B

C

1993

D

E

A

B

1994

C

D

E

F

G

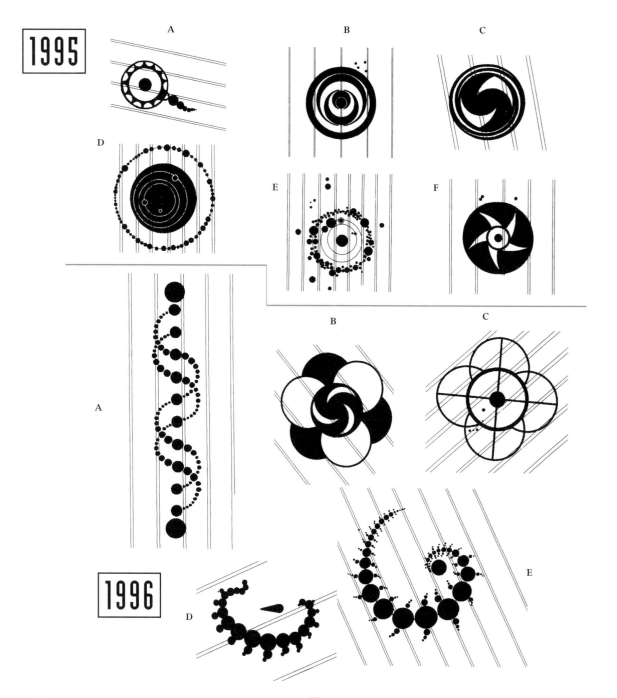

1995

A

B

C

D

E

F

1996

A

B

C

D

E

A

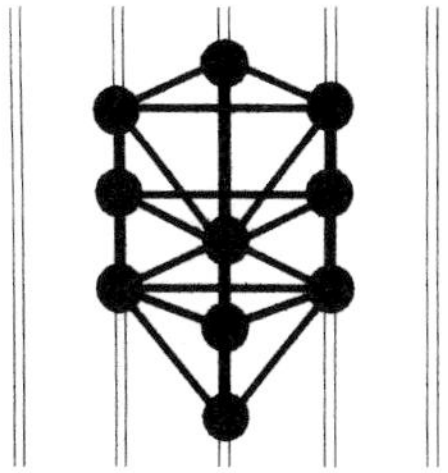

B

C

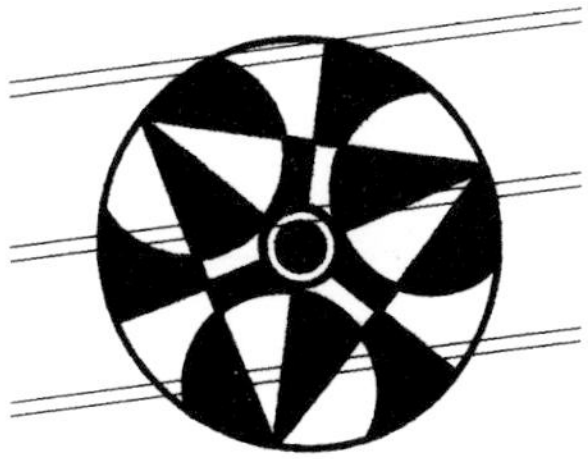

D

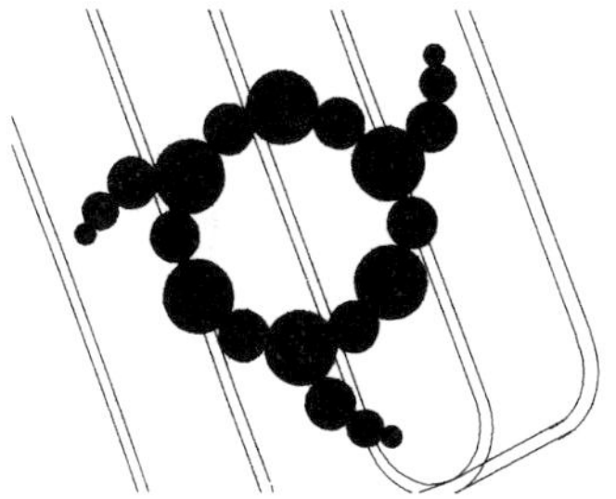

F

E

G

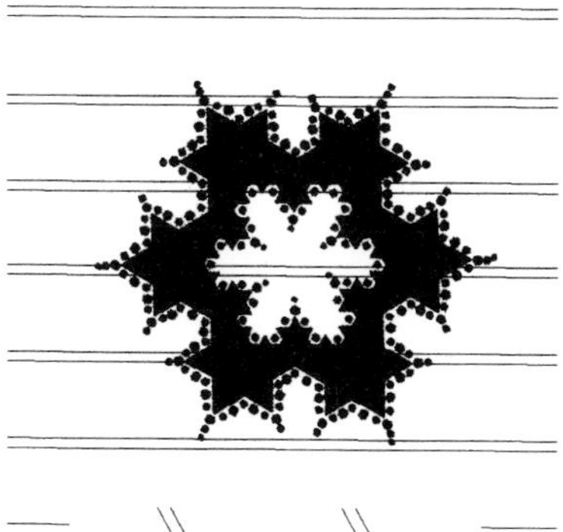

H

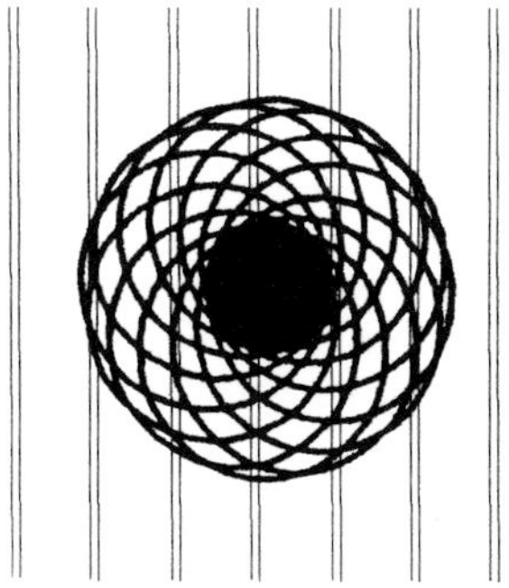

1997

I

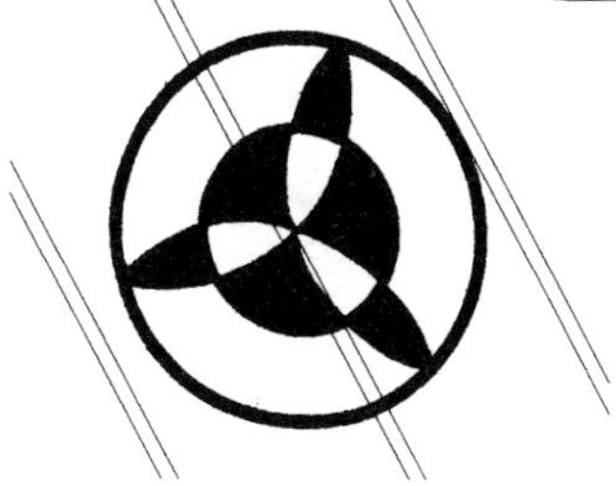

J

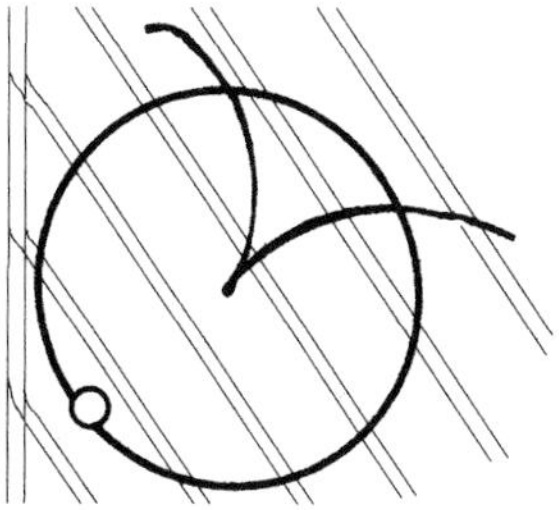

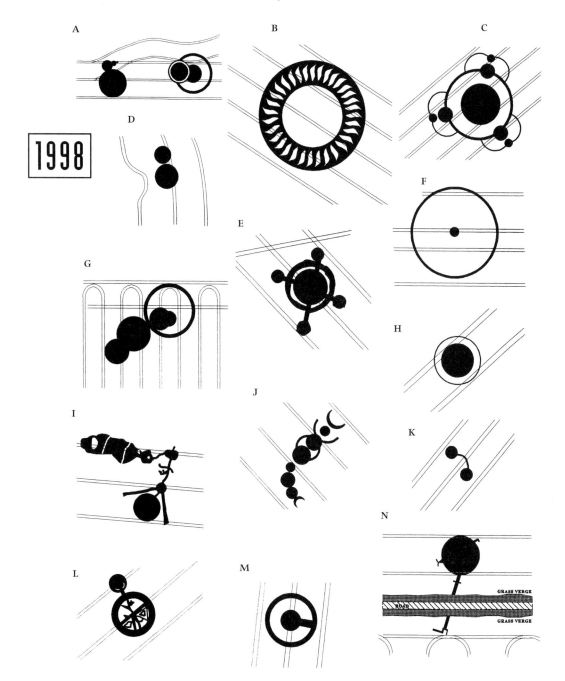

1998

A

B

C

D

E

F

G

H

I

J

K

L

M

N

GRASS VERGE

ROAD

GRASS VERGE

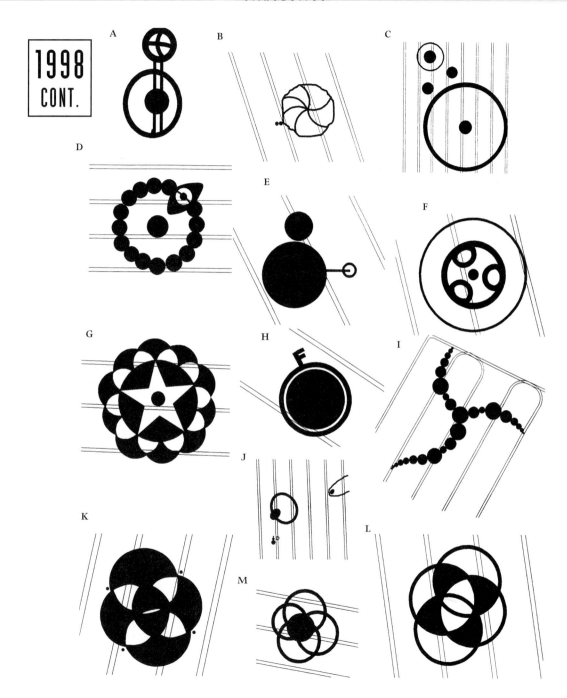

A

B

C

D

E

F

G

H

I

J

K

M

L

1998
CONT.

1998 CONT.

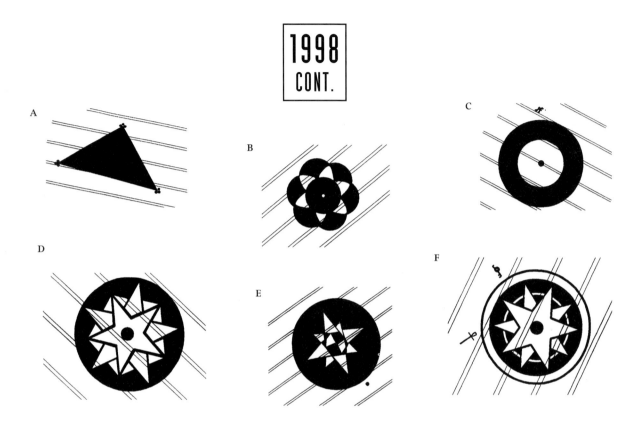

A

B

C

D

E

F

ALL SILHOUETTES DRAWN TO SCALE.

© Nigel Tomsett and Debbie Pardoe

Author's Note

I do hope that people who have read this book will send me reports of any strange or unusual happenings, not just related to the circles, ancient monuments or sites (there is evidence that there is a link between the ancient places and the circles), but of other strange experiences and happenings for which they can find no rational explanation. Nothing is too small or insignificant, and I would like to reassure everyone that they will remain anonymous unless permission has been given otherwise, and I will honour everything told me in confidence.

For photographs, calendars and other crop circle goods, please send an SAE to:

Lucy Pringle
5 Town Lane
Sheet
Petersfield
Hampshire GU32 2AF

Tel/Fax: +44 (0)1730 263454
Email: LucyPringle@compuserve.com.

Bibliography

AAIB Bulletin No. 3/94, *AAIB Field Investigation*, ref: EW/C93/8/2, 1993

Alexandersson, Olof, *Living Water: Vicktor Schauberger and the Secrets of Natural Energy*, Gateway, Bath, 1990

Backster, Cleve and White, Stephen G., of Backster Research Inc. San Diego, 'Biocommunication Capability at a Distance between Human Donors and Invitro Oral Leukocytes', unpublished report presented at the Cosmos Club, Washington DC, 3 September 1985, and at the Fall Scientific Meeting of the Orthomolecular Medical Society, San Francisco CA, 18 November 1985.

Bartholomew, Alick (ed.), *Harbingers of World Change*, Gateway, Bath, 1991

Bennett, Mary and Percy, David, *Dark Moon, Apollo and the Whistle Blowers*, Aulis, London, 1999

Bentine, Michael, *Open Your Mind*, Corgi Books, 1992

Blackmore, Susan, 'The Inside Story', in *New Scientist*, November, 1994

Briggs, Katherine, *The Fairies in English Tradition and Literature*, Bellew Publishing, London, 1989

Burl, Aubrey, *Prehistoric Avebury*, BCA, London, 1979

Collinge, William, *Subtle Energy*, Thorsons, London, 1998

Collins, Andrew, *The Circlemakers*, ABC Books, Leigh-on-Sea, 1992

Davies, Beth (ed.), *Ciphers in the Crops*, Gateway, Bath, 1992

Cyr, Donald L., *Crop Circle Secrets*, Stonehenge Viewpoint, 1991

Dames, Michael, *The Silbury Treasure*, Thames and Hudson, London, 1992

Delgado, P. *Conclusive Evidence*, Bloomsbury, London, 1992

Delgado, P. and Andrews, Colin, *Circular Evidence*, Bloomsbury, London, 1989

Delgado, P. and Andrews, Colin, *The Latest Evidence*, Bloomsbury, London, 1992

Dickens, Charles, *Bleak House* (revised edition), Penguin, London, 1996

Eade, Peter, *Paranormal Pranks*, Pringle, Petersfield, 1996

Gerber, Richard, *Vibrational Medicine*, Bear & Co., Santa Fe, 1988

Glickman, Michael, *Corn Circles*, Woden Books, Presteigne, Wales, 1996

Goodman, Kent, *Crop Circles of Wessex*, Wessex Books, Salisbury, 1996

Hall, Manly P., *The Secret Teaching of All Ages*, The Philosophical Research Society, Los Angeles, 1977

Hampshire Federation of Women's Institutes, *The New Hampshire Village Book*, Countryside Books, Newbury, 1990

Heseman, Michael, *The Cosmic Connection*, Gateway, Bath, 1996

Hope, Murray, *Atlantis, Myth or Reality?* Arkana, London, 1991

Jung, Carl, *Memories, Dreams, Reflections*, Flamingo, London, 1983

Kaptchuk, Ted J., *The Web that has no Weaver*, Congdon and Weed, New York, 1983

Keen, Montague, *1991 – Scientific Evidence for the Crop Circle Phenomenon*, Elvery Dowers Publications, Norwich, 1992

Macnish, John, *Crop Circle Apocalypse*, Circlevision, 1993

Martineau, John, *Crop Circle Geometry,* Woden Books, Presteigne, Wales, 1992

Marshman, Michael, *The Wiltshire Village Book,* Countryside Books, Newbury, 1990

Maxwell-Cade, C. and Coxhead, Nona, *The Awakening Mind*, Element Books, Shaftesbury, 1991

Meaden, Terence, *The Crop Circle Effect and its Mysteries,* Artech, London, 1989

Meaden, Terence, *Circles from the Sky*, Souvenir Press, London, 1991

Meaden, Terence, *The Goddess of the Stones and the Stonehenge Solution*, Souvenir Press, London, 1991

Michell, John (ed.), *Dowsing the Crop Circles,* Gothic Image, Glastonbury, 1991

Morton, Chris and Thomas, Ceri Louise, *The Mystery of the Crystal Skulls*, Thorsons, London, 1997

Miller, Hamish and Broadbent, Paul, *The Sun and The Serpent,* Pendragon Press, Launceston, 1991

Myers, P. and Percy, David, *Two Thirds*, Aulis, London, 1993

Noyes, Ralph (ed.), *The Crop Circle Enigma*, Gateway, Bath, 1990

Palgrave-Moore, Pat, *Crop Circle Classification*, Elvery Dowers Publications, Norwich, 1991

Pratchett, Terry, *Lords and Ladies*, Corgi Books, London, 1993

Randles, Jenny and Fuller, Paul, *Crop Circles: A Mystery Solved*, Robert Hale, 1990

Rickard, Bob, 'Rings of Ice', *The Fortean Times*, No. 74 April/May 1994.

Roney-Dougal, Serena, *Where Science and Magic Meet*, Element Books, Shaftesbury, 1993

Ruby, Doug, *The Gift*, Blue Note Books, Cape Canaveral, 1995

Schlemmer, Phyllis (ed.) with Jenkins, Palden, *The Only Planet of Choice*, Gateway, Bath, 1993

Schnabel, Jim, *Round in Circles*, Penguin, London, 1993

Schiff, Michel, *The Memory of Water*, Thorsons, London, 1995

Sheldrake, Rupert, *The Presence of the Past*, Fontana, London, 1989

Stannard, Russell, *The Space and Time of Uncle Albert*, Faber and Faber, London, 1990

Stannard, Russell, *Black Holes and Uncle Albert*, Faber and Faber, London, 1992

Stannard, Russell, *Here I Am*, Faber and Faber, London, 1993

Stannard, Russell, *World of 1001 Mysteries,* Faber and Faber, London, 1993

Strainic, Michael, 'Once Upon a Time in the Wheat', in *Mufon UFO Journal*, No. 284, December 1991

Talbot, Michael, *Holographic Universe*, Haper Perennial, New York, 1992

Taylor, Busty, *Crop Circles of 1991*, Beckhampton Books, Beckhampton, 1992

Bibliography

Thomas, Andy, *Fields of Mystery*, SB Publications, Seaford, East Sussex, 1996

Thomas, Andy, *Vital Signs*, SB Publications, Seaford, East Sussex, 1998

Thomas, Andy and Bura, Paul, *Quest for Contact*, SB Publications, Seaford, East Sussex, 1997

Toffler, Alvin, *Future Shock*, Bantam, New York, 1971

Vigay Paul, 'Crop Circle Hoaxing: is it a threat to the genuine phenomenon?', unpublished report, 1994

Wakelam, Keith, *Discovering Eternity,* Mulberry Books, Calais, France, 1986

Whitlock, Ralph, *Wiltshire Folklore and Legend*, Robert Hale, 1992

Wiltshire, Kathleen, *Ghosts and Legends of the Wiltshire Countryside*, Colin Venton Ltd, Melksham, 1985

Williams, Margot and Morgan, Carolyn, *The Answer*, Grosvenor Press, London, 1991

Wilson, Terry, *The Secret History of Crop Circles*, CCCS, Paignton, Devon, 1998

Zim, Herbert S. and Baker, Robert H., *Stars*, Paul Hamlyn, London, 1965

Readers may be surprised to find Russell Stannard's science books for children included in the bibliography. I found his explanations of complicated concepts both illuminating and simple to grasp. They provide an excellent foundation.

Index

Index